D0378721

JAN 0 4 1993	3/19/97	
FEB 1 2 1994 MAR 2 0 1996		
3/8/94	AUG 1 9 1998	
NOV 2 6 1994		
DEC 0 8 1994		
DEC 1 2 1994		
MAY 2 0 1995		
JUN 1 2 1995		
JUL 3 1 1995		
8/31/95		
FEB 2 6 1996		
MAR 1 8 1996		
MAY 0 4 1996		
FEB 2 4 1997		

ADULT ART PSYCHOTHERAPY

Issues and Applications

ADULT

ART

PSYCHOTHERAPY

Issues and Applications

Edited by

Helen B. Landgarten
M.A., A.T.R., H.L.M.
Professor Emeritus, Loyola Marymount University

and

Darcy Lubbers
M.A., A.T.R.

BRUNNER/MAZEL, *Publishers* • New York

Library of Congress Cataloging-in-Publication Data
Adult art psychotherapy : issues and applications / edited by Helen B.
Landgarten and Darcy Lubbers.
   p.   cm.
Includes bibliographical references.
ISBN 0-87630-593-1
1. Art therapy. I. Landgarten, Helen B. II. Lubbers, Darcy.
[DNLM: 1. Art Therapy. WM 450.5.AB A2435]
RC489.A7A36 1991
616.89'1656—dc20
DNLM/DLC
for Library of Congress   90–15103
                                              CIP

Copyright © 1991 by Brunner/Mazel, Inc.

Published by
BRUNNER/MAZEL, INC.
19 Union Square West
New York, New York 10003

Manufactured in the United States of America

10 9 8 7 6 5 4 3 2 1

To Loyola Marymount University
and
Immaculate Heart College

With everlasting appreciation for laying the educational foundation for Clinical Art Therapy on the west coast. This book would not have come into being without their faith and support.

Contents

About the Editors

HELEN B. LANDGARTEN, M.A., A.T.R., H.L.M.

Helen B. Landgarten pioneered art psychotherapy on the west coast. In 1967, as a senior staff member of Cedars-Sinai Medical Center in the Family/Child Department of Psychiatry, she introduced the art therapy modality for diagnosis and treatment. In 1974 the position of Coordinator of Art Psychotherapy was designated for her and she still serves in that capacity to this day.

In 1972, she founded and directed the Clinical Art Therapy Master Degree Program, first at Immaculate Heart College, later at Loyola Marymount University. Landgarten is currently a Professor Emeritus at the latter institution and continues to be a faculty member.

Recognized for her outstanding contribution to the field, she was given the award of an Honorary Life Member in both the American Art Therapy Association and the Southern Art Therapy Association. Landgarten has given paper presentations, lectures, and workshops in many countries throughout the world. She is listed nationally and internationally in over thirty *Who's Who* editions and has been interviewed on a large number of television programs. Throughout the years, newspapers in various cities have presented featured articles about Mrs. Landgarten and her innovative work. Included in a long list of publications are two books: *Clinical Art Therapy: A Comprehensive Guide* (1980) and *Family Art Psychotherapy: A Clinical Guide and Casebook* (1987). Helen Landgarten currently exhibits her own artwork, acts as an international art psychotherapy consultant, and is writing two books: *The Synergistic Approach to Creative Art and Writing*, and *Collage as a Diagnostic and Treatment Tool*.

DARCY LUBBERS, M.A., A.T.R.

Darcy Lubbers is in private practice in Beverly Hills, California, working with individuals with a wide variety of presenting problems. She has had extensive experience in the treatment of eating disorders, and as early as 1982, she instituted art therapy as part of a treatment program at the Woodview Calabasas Psychiatric Hospital, Los Angeles. Ms. Lubbers is an eating disorders consultant to various hospitals in the greater Los Angeles area. She is also known for her work in alcohol and substance abuse and in relationship counseling, for "women who rescue men." Ms. Lubbers currently serves as a supervisor of students for the Graduate Department of Clinical Art Therapy at Loyola Marymount University.

About the Contributors

ANN DILLHOEFER BUSSARD, M.A., A.T.R.

Ann Bussard established a pioneering program in clinical art therapy that provides services to AIDS and cancer patients in the St. Vincent Medical Center, and also to a residential AIDS shelter in the Los Angeles area. Her clinical experience also includes conducting art therapy groups in the Pasadena schools through the auspices of San Gabriel Valley Mental Health Education Foundation. Mrs. Bussard is currently working as the Program Director of the Wellness Community-Foothills, a free support program for cancer patients and their family members. She is in private practice in Los Angeles.

JULIA GENTLEMAN BYERS, M.A., A.T.R.

Julia Gentleman Byers, Assistant Professor, is currently the Director of Graduate Studies in Art Therapy Programmes at Concordia University in Montreal, Quebec, Canada. Her diverse clinical background includes experience in outpatient clinics, in residential adolescent treatment and assessment facilities, special education programs in school systems, and in private practice with children, young adults, and families. She has worked as a clinical art therapist in Los Angeles, Toronto, and Montreal for the past 10 years.

MIRIAM ELLINGSON, M.A.

Miriam Ellingson has worked extensively as an art therapist with the mentally and physically disabled in Santa Cruz, California. She has also been involved in the San Francisco Zen Center's Hospice Organization. Ms. Ellingson has made numerous trips to the Soviet Union, under the auspices of the Center for U.S./U.S.S.R. initiatives; in September, 1988, she led a tour of twenty Americans through Moscow, Leningrad, and Vilnius, Lithuania as part of a "twelve step" project entitled "Creating a Sober World." Currently living in Marin County, she is painting and studying philosophy.

SUSAN KLEINMAN, M.A.

Susan Kleinman established one of the first art therapy treatment programs in the country for AIDS patients. She began with the AIDS Project at the Hollywood Community Hospital, in the Immune Suppressed Unit. Her agency experience also includes the West Covina Hospital Chemical Dependency Unit and the Pacific Clinics Children's Day Treatment Program, both in Los Angeles.

DIANE SILVERMAN, M.A., A.T.R.

Diane Silverman is on the faculty of the Graduate Department of Clinical Art Therapy at Loyola Marymount University as both instructor and supervisor. Since 1978, she has served as an art therapy consultant at Westwood Hospital, working with adults and adolescents in both individual and group treatment. Numerous papers on art therapy have been presented by Ms. Silverman at mental health facilities, psychiatric hospitals, and conferences. She is in private practice in West Los Angeles.

SANDRA STARK SHIELDS, M.A., A.T.R.

Sandra Stark Shields has had vast experience in working with dysfunctional families. She is currently treating sexually and physically abused children and their families at Pacific Clinics, Los Angeles. She has also worked with family violence in other outpatient and inpatient settings, including Los Angeles Family Counseling Services, and Northridge Hospital Medical Center. Mrs. Stark Shields is a faculty member and supervisor at the Graduate Clinical Art Therapy program at Loyola Marymount University.

Foreword

Adult Art Psychotherapy, edited by Helen Landgarten and Darcy Lubbers, illuminates the range and ever-expanding nature of art therapy as it completes its first two decades of formal existence. In their introduction the editors suggest that clinical art therapy is capable of adapting to different theories and methods of therapy and that it is equally facile in responding to the diverse problems, opportunities, and changes in adult life. Helen Landgarten has systematically applied herself to documenting the spectrum of art therapy practice in this volume and in her two previous books, *Clinical Art Therapy* (1981) and *Family Art Psychotherapy* (1987). Rather than looking at life and the practice of therapy through a fixed theory or method, she is more interested in responding to what presents itself. Art therapy emerges as a protean process which is ongoing and forever revitalizing itself through its versatility.

In addition to presenting examples of diversity through detailed descriptions of the work of the eight art therapists who contribute chapters to this book, the editors encourage readers to continue the creative process by making their own applications. They assure us that art therapy will always generate new methods because it "is synergistic with practically any goal or approach."

The first chapter by Miriam Ellingson looks at art therapy from a philosophical perspective and affirms our profession's deep and compassionate connections to "fundamental facts of human existence." The discipline of "clinical philosophy" can be good medicine for art therapy and it will help us to continuously reexamine assumptions about health and illness as well as the ideas on which we base methods of treatment. This chapter's revisioning of psychopathology and art through existentialism and phenomenology sets the context for the five following chapters in which the authors show how they use art to treat some of the pathologies of our era: suicide (Julia Gentleman Byers), women with eating disorders (Darcy Lubbers), borderline personality organization (Diane Silverman), mothers of incestuously abused children (Sandra Stark Shields) and AIDS (Ann Bussard and Susan Kleinman). The authors' methods vary and reflect the varieties of practice that we find in art therapy today. They range from drawing assessments adapted from psychological testing, which assume that images can be reduced to particular psychological conditions that afflict the artist (an aspect of art therapy that does not arouse my personal enthusiasm but which nevertheless attracts many people), to the use of expressive art as a supportive way to help AIDS patients to sustain their "struggle for life."

All of the authors, although expressing differences of style and interpretive philosophies, affirm the ability of the artistic process to communicate emotions and psychic conditions that simply cannot be accessed through rational and linear language. This essential aspect of art therapy finds itself being widely understood in the world today. Just recently on the morning news I heard that the children of men and women in the U.S. military who had been sent to the Persian Gulf were asked to draw pictures in school about the feelings they were experiencing because teachers found that it was not possible to talk directly about these complex and varied psychological losses, fears, and fantasies. But where adult society has been quick to adapt to the use of art to further communication of childrens' psychic states, it has been less responsive to becoming involved itself. We have yet to correct the general attitude that drawings are fine for children, but not for grown-ups. Our adult inclination to talk about feelings simultaneously limits us to the habits and controlled patterns of speech. Art therapy with adults offers a direct and multifaceted mode of embodying emotional conditions that will often become visible to the person for the first time through painting. The ability of images to reveal themselves automatically *through the process of expression* is what distinguishes art from expressive modes that communicate thoughts already known to the person. In addition to the expansion of communication, art therapy offers adults the chance to regain worlds of imagination and creative expression that we have previously restricted to children.

In the last chapter of the book, Helen Landgarten complements the breadth orientation of the preceding chapters by demonstrating how an art therapist carefully observes, organizes, and reflects upon her experience with one man over the course of the entire therapeutic experience. The theme of this chapter is termination and the last phase of therapy. The description of how she and the client review the art from previous sessions is more than a presentation of a therapeutic technique. By describing the review of art and showing the man's "self-recorded treatment process" and the changes resulting from the work of the "client's own hands," Landgarten has found a way to present an engaging and consolidated account of the therapy with Mr. Tate. The art review demonstrates how art therapy is a kinetic experience through which images and people change in relation to one another and their environments.

Adult Art Psychotherapy is a tribute to the achievements of the graduate program in clinical art therapy that Helen Landgarten founded at Immaculate Heart College in 1973 and moved to Loyola Marymount University in Los

Angeles in 1980. All of the contributors are graduates of the program. As one of the people involved in the first phases of art therapy education and training I never imagined that our solitary efforts to establish graduate programs would have such far-reaching influences and unimagined spin-offs. I am continuously delighted to see how the profession attracts gifted and dedicated men and women who dream of making art therapy their life work, and I am impressed to see how people, like the contributors to this book, have succeeded in arousing the curiosity and winning the respect of colleagues in other health disciplines. The accomplishments of the Loyola Marymount community correspond to what other large and small groups of art therapists are doing throughout the United States and the world. This volume takes a large step in affirming our ability to expand and change the way mental health services are provided. It will add to the ongoing process of creative multiplication that I see occuring in art therapy.

I look forward to the day when the influences that we are having on the medical, educational, and human services fields will go full circle and change the broader context of art and life. Many of us are refugees and immigrants from art's elitist and nonsynergistic modus operandi, which has not since the revolutionary days of the surrealists provided opportunities for engaging the depths of psyche. Desiring to relate art to something other than itself, we have settled in the terrain of psychotherapy and we have found it to be fertile ground for realizing our personal and social objectives as artists who want to assist people who suffer and long for creative changes in their lives. Synergism acknowledges the importance of the archetypal pair, cooperative agencies, and combinations that work together and stimulate participants to create new relationships. As C. G. Jung said, "the One is never separated from the Other." This book urges art therapy to shape itself through endless cooperations and pairings as contrasted to the tendency to define ourselves through opposition and separation from other disciplines.

Art therapy is an expression of that aspect of art which longs for connection to life. It never ceases in its striving to relate creatively and emotionally with the other. *Adult Art Psychotherapy* clearly documents the success of what has been done over the relatively brief period of two decades of art therapy history. I wish the authors and their readers well in furthering this "synergistic" philosophy of collaboration and creative relationships that might someday take us home to art as full participants in its life.

SHAUN MCNIFF, Ph.D.
Professor, Lesley Graduate School
Cambridge, Massachusetts

Introduction

Although the profession of art therapy has taken gigantic strides since the inception of the American Art Therapy Association in 1969, it is still a relatively young and growing field with rapidly expanding definitions. At the present time, while the public is still learning about the very existence of art psychotherapy as a viable source of treatment, psychotherapists of all disciplines are seriously seeking to gain their own knowledge of this subject.

Therefore, it is the intent of this volume not only to give an update on the important work that is being done in the field, but also to reveal the breadth and scope of adult art psychotherapy. The chapters in this book, written by experts on specific issues related to art therapy treatment for adults, were purposefully chosen to give a fuller picture of the numerous possibilities for working with the art therapy model.

In the opening chapter, Miriam Ellingson applies ideas from a new movement—Clinical Philosophy—to art therapy. Clinical Philosophy addresses psychological suffering by recognizing that it is related to ontological anxiety. Drawing from her work with physically and psychologically disabled adults, Ellingson presents a paradigm of six existential sources of anxiety and integrates them into the art therapy process. The author challenges art therapists to apply existentialism and phenomenology in their practices.

In the second chapter, Julia Byers explores the relevance of adult developmental theories of identity crisis and transitions to the study of suicide. She presents vignettes of both hospitalized and outpatient clients and their image-making processes and also discusses metaphors as a means to understanding underlying messages. Byers takes a dynamically oriented stance in working with suicidal persons.

Further demonstrating the diversity of art therapy, Chapters 3, 4, 5, and 6 highlight its strong potential in the treatment of various specific populations. In Chapter 3, Darcy Lubbers describes the treatment approach she has formulated for working with women suffering from the eating disorders of anorexia nervosa and bulimia nervosa. She elucidates the important role that the clinical art therapist plays in the milieu treatment approach of these disorders. The artwork throughout this chapter provides an evocative testimony to the inner lives of these patients.

Diane Silverman, in the fourth chapter, presents a synthesized theory of borderline psychopathology, along with implications for art psychotherapy treatment utilizing these concepts. A proposal is made that art psychotherapy provides an entry into the internal world of these patients in a particular way that may not be possible by other means. Based upon her extensive experience with hospitalized patients, Silverman describes the use of art psychotherapy as a "holding environment" for individuals who experience themselves on the dangerous edge of fragmentation. In addition, it can enhance the quality of the interaction and the therapeutic work within the transference.

Sandra Stark Shields, in Chapter 5, describes her work with a group of mothers whose children have been incestuously abused. She examines the dynamics and treatment issues in these families, focuses on the role of the mother, and describes the catalytic effect of the art directives and the treatment procedures for group work.

One of the most tragic problems of our time is the focus of Chapter 6. Acquired Immune Deficiency Syndrome (AIDS) is a devastating disease, with intense emotional repercussions. Ann Bussard and Susan Kleinman present their methods of group and individual treatment with AIDS patients. They explain the use of contrasting art tasks in helping patients to ventilate their negative feelings and explore day-to-day coping methods and sources of life-extending support and hope. Some of the artwork remains as a lasting testament and tribute to the individuality, human dignity, and creativity of the producers who have since died.

The closing chapter of this book is significant on several levels. Helen Landgarten offers a review of the factors that influence the last phase of treatment—termination—leading the reader through the powerful experience of a retrospective artwork summary, which in part focuses on the events and feelings that were dealt with in therapy. In the next part of this process, Landgarten explains the progression of body imagery drawings as analogous to emotional growth and the autonomy of the client as she or he steps out of the therapy context. Last, the author describes the review as valuable not only for the client, but for the therapist as well.

Taken as a whole, *Adult Art Psychotherapy* is an informative update on work being done in the field, which provides numerous applications and current thought across a broad spectrum of issues. The book explores what's happening now—and what's possible for the future. As clinical art therapy is synergistic with practically any goal or approach, it is our hope that mental health professionals who read this book will consider creative ways of incorporating their own modes of therapy to the issues, theories, and applications contained herein.

HELEN B. LANDGARTEN
DARCY LUBBERS

ADULT ART PSYCHOTHERAPY

Issues and Applications

Chapter 1

A Philosophy for Clinical Art Therapy

Miriam Ellingson

Many clients treated with conventional therapy are likely to be suffering from philosophical conditions rooted in the individual's existence rather than psychological diseases. A relatively new movement in psychology has evolved from philosophy and goes by several names such as humanistic psychology, existential psychology, or clinical philosophy. Clinical philosophy is a formalization of the relationship between the application of philosophy to psychotherapy. This chapter applies some of the relevant aspects of clinical philosophy to art therapy.

I was greatly influenced by Peter Koestenbaum's work and writings in clinical philosophy, most thoroughly formulated in his book *The New Image of the Person* (1978). Historically, art therapy has modeled itself after the various models of treatment in the field of psychology and psychiatry, beginning with Freud. Such trends grew out of the scientific and medical models where the emphasis is on treatment and are based on categorizing kinds and degrees of mental illness and neurosis. My approach comes from the field of existential philosophy, the philosophy of the twentieth century, with its emphasis on the human being living in the world and dealing with ultimate existential concerns, not necessarily secondary and tertiary symptoms that define experience only in objective terms.

There are many authors in the field of psychology and psychiatry who have published works on existential philosophy and its application to clinical work, for example, William Ofman (1976), Irving Yalom (1980), J. H. Van Den Berg (1972), Rollo May (1958), and James Bugenthal (1978). Yalom (1980) believes experienced clinicians often operate implicitly within an existential framework. He claims that "major existential concerns have been recognized and discussed since the beginning of written thought, and their primacy has been recognized by an unbroken stream of philosophers, theologians, and poets" (p. 12). One philosopher, Joseph Campbell, supports this view: "The secret cause of all suffering . . . is mortality itself . . ." (1988, p. xiii).

Clinical philosophy addresses psychological suffering by recognizing that our most basic suffering is, as R. D. Laing (1962) says, "ontological insecurity." This is suffering where the individual lacks a sense of self, of the permanency of things or the substantiality of others and natural processes. Koestenbaum (1978) addresses this suffering in terms of three philosophical facts: first, a consciousness world stream runs through each human being; the second philosophical fact is the converse of one—the decision to constitute an individual identity from this universal stream; and the third philosophical fact is a synthesis of the foregoing two polar characteristics of being. This unifying position shows that life is not a permanent decision, either for universality or individuality. It is the conflict between the ambiguity and stress that these poles embody that actually allow the experience of feeling alive, of existing and being. The ensuing struggle that occurs as the individual emerges from the universal sea of consciousness is the experience of existential anxiety.

This theory of the personality is presented in this chapter in terms of the anxieties that are the universal problems of living. Clinical philosophy theory illuminates the relationship between philosophy and humanistic psychology. It enters the clinical, counseling, or therapeutic setting where, if it is said that ultimate existential concerns never arise, it is only because the therapist may either not be sensitive to hearing these concerns or believes that because they are universal experiences, nothing beneficial can come from their exploration.

Shaun McNiff and Mala Betensky are art therapists who have seen the usefulness of the phenomenological/existential perspective. McNiff (1973) addresses the phenomenological approach "based upon the conviction that a one-sided involvement with the often vague and confusing unconscious features of the art experience fails to maximize the therapeutic potential of an analysis of objective pictorial dynamics." He goes on to state, "We (teachers and staff) emphasize the importance of distinguishing between what is objectively present in perception and the subjective feelings of the viewer" (p. 243). This emphasis is not only important for those with perceptual difficulties or crippled consciousnesses, but necessary to us all as descriptions of our relatedness within the dialectic field of being.

Betensky (1977) focuses on the client's artwork process and art expression as phenomena of consciousness. She warns of the eagerness of art therapists to apply complex theory into oversimplified or ready-made techniques, thereby distorting theorists' original concepts—which has happened, particularly with Jung and Freud. She outlines a theoretical structure for art therapy which is independent of prevalent approaches, including attachments to the "creative process itself." She feels these ideas could provide a viable new direction for understanding the process of self-discovery through art expression.

ART THERAPY INTEGRATED INTO CLINICAL PHILOSOPHY

I apply ideas from clinical philosophy to art therapy because they are analogous to the art process. In the art process there is the experience of struggling to establish equilibrium between polarities. Between the polarities of the conception of an idea in the creative experience to the formation of a final product there is a place where opposition, alternation, and otherness exist, all striving for preservation and fulfillment. May (1975) describes this encounter by saying, "Knowledge itself—as well as poetry, art, and other creative products— arises out of the dynamic encounter between subjective and objective poles" (p. 98). The continuous back and forth struggle between polarities breeds vitality into creation. May also postulates the following:

> Our traditional psychology has been founded on the dichotomy between subject and object which has been the central characteristic of Western thought for the past four centuries. Ludwig Binswanger calls this dichotomy, "the cancer of all psychology and psychiatry up to now." It is not avoided by behaviorism or operationalism, which would define experience only in objective terms. Nor is it avoided by isolating the creative experience as purely subjective phenomenon. (1975, pp. 49–50)

May (1975) claims that we have set reason over emotion, believing we can observe something more accurately if emotions are left out. However, data in Rorschach responses indicate that people see more sharply and more accurately when emotions are engaged. An object cannot really be seen without some subjective emotional involvement with it.

In an effort to establish equilibrium with respect to the art experience, art therapist Janie Rhyne (1977) says, "In my view, art therapists, art educators, aestheticians, and those psychologists interested in art tend to emphasize the emotional impact and empathy in art experience and to step gingerly around its cognitive orientation" (p. 93).

There has been much debate within the field over How much art? How much therapy? How important the process? How important the product? How much creativity? How much verbalization? Perhaps we can accept the fact that art therapy is bound for its existence to be constantly defined and redefined as life itself, considering that the people within the field come from the art world where established systems are constantly being examined, changed, or destroyed. Something of Albert Camus's that I heard a long time ago applies here, which advises us that "the aim of art just as the aim of a life can only be to increase the sum of freedom and responsibility to be found in every person and in the world."

Discrimination between mental and emotional processes in art therapy is not necessary. Perceptions are not necessarily closer to self-knowledge than conception. What is important is to know what one believes. Artwork in a supportive environment can evoke whole-body thinking, it can activate consciousness between the polarities of individual and world, subject and object, mind and body. Koestenbaum (1987) states that "self-expression is much more than it first appears to be. It has to do with the important philosophic and psychological concepts of grounding" (pp. 19–20). The "work" of art, as is each individual being, can be the interface between inner and outer world, between the spiritual and the material.

To summarize this philosophical approach to the art process: I am, as you are, a conscious inward and subjective center and a body confronted at all times with objective reality consisting of other conscious centers, society, and nature. Within this field we are on the one hand to participate, get involved, and identify with emotions and actions, and on the other hand we reflect, detach and distance from them when we choose. The art process is the struggle with objective reality, the participation in life, the identification and involvement with thoughts, feelings, and actions, and the creation of ourselves as individuals. The art product and verbal associations to it are the reflection, the stepping back, the psychic distancing, and bracketing of experience, as well as the disengagement of the empirical ego to the experience of the transcendental consciousness that runs through us.

As previously mentioned, symptoms of the polar structure of being are our conflicts and anxieties. How we cope with the ambiguities and inconsistencies inherent in this dialectic, in general, determines how we manage its specific instances. Yalom (1980) states, "These existential sources of dread are familiar, too, in that they are the experience of the therapist as Everyman; they are by no means the exclusive province of the psychologically troubled individual" (p. 12).

Anxiety in an existential sense is healthy, normal, and desirable, as well as revelatory of our problems of living in terms of the subject-object field. A denial of existential anxieties (i.e., repression, rationalization, reaction formation) is a denial of our nature and becomes neurotic anxiety—a denial of insights and truths about ourselves. This denial can produce physical symptoms such as high blood pressure, behavioral symptoms such as alcoholism, and psychological symptoms such as depression. Neurotic anxiety is also fear of anxiety itself, anxiety over being anxious, similar to being afraid of being afraid. Koestenbaum (1976) states,

When we are anxious, we experience the truth about ourselves and the world. But when we are anxious about being anxious, then we are sick and needlessly limit our potential for enjoying living and appreciating reality. (p. 56)

Anxiety reveals different sources of insights. If an individual feels anxious, he or she may be experiencing one or a combination of these fundamental facts of human existence. I present here the use of a paradigm of existential sources of anxiety and dread, differentiating them and integrating six of these sources into the art therapy process. None are psychological problems but, rather, ancient and universal problems of living. They are the anxieties of freedom, individuality, birth, evil, nihilism, and death.

Freedom

This brings us to the matter of freedom and its resulting anxiety. In a 1978 lecture I heard Rollo May describe freedom as the pause that breaks into cause and effect—a phenomenology of total self, not just intellect. In the framework of clinical philosophy the patients and clients learn that with this freedom we construct our world—that the experience of freedom is the experience of consciousness. The experience of consciousness is an infinite backward movement illuminating the world and our freedom to create our own world.

An example of the freedom to constitute our life in the art therapy process is demonstrated when a person makes a scribble with one color and then with other colors brings out the images found therein. The scribble and the art media are symbolic of the amorphous, monochromatic objects which we become aware of some time after conception. The choice of colors and the evolved forms that become the final product symbolize how, with alternative choices and decision making, we gradually constitute a complete three-dimensional world of which we are the sum product.

A diagnosis of loss of access to one's freedom can be made when the client continually uses the same one or two colors, repeatedly draws only on a small part of the page, and restricts his or her use of forms and texture. Therapy for this diagnosis might be that these pictures be saved and later reviewed with the client, thus serving as reminder of how he or she had chosen a particular color, form, and subject. The art therapist could also ask the client to make his or her verbal associations to the product, reminding the client of his or her responsibility for it, perhaps preceded with the words, "I chose to use one color to make this image, and then I chose this form, and I chose to leave the page empty . . .," and so forth.

My work in a convalescent hospital with geriatric patients who had lost many of their senses is another illustration of the anxiety of freedom, and its treatment, in art therapy. I attempted to get these patients to use any ounce of freedom that they still had. Lila, for example, was 97 years old and confined to a wheelchair. She had very little hearing or vision capability, and her hands lay uselessly in her lap, crippled from arthritis. I would hold up cut-out magazine pictures close to Lila and she would choose two or three images. They were then pasted onto a brightly colored piece of construction paper. I allowed the patient to choose where I would glue the pictures. After this, I would take her hand in mine and with a black marker title each picture according to her desire.

One might say, Why bother with these old, mentally or physically disabled people? The only way I can answer that question is to say that Lila is a human being; not many things touch her awareness or evoke in her a sense of freedom, but she is still choosing to remain alive. When she worked with me on her picture, her face got red, she attempted to verbalize (normally she did not), and her head would move to look up at me, a simple but exhausting effort for her. In other words, Lila became more alive, if only for a short while.

Recognizing the interconnectedness of all beings as part of the stream of consciousness, I acknowledge with deep respect any spark of awareness that remains. In working with mentally or physically ill people, making a picture together can establish trust and friendship. This act alone touches their freedom by helping them overcome their apparent decision to permanently isolate themselves from existence, and this isolation puts their freedom to disuse. The art therapy environment itself can entice a person to utilize more of his or her freedom.

Creativity and the constitution of each life are, in my mind, synonymous terms. In creating a picture, the givens are the media. In constituting a life, the givens are the world of objects. In both acts there is the fear of disapproval. Anxiety is provoked when we realize that we create, choose, mold, and invent our universe out of nothingness. This realization of our freedom is in continuous battle with anxiety; but if freedom is too constricted, the creator will die and the constitutor's potential will go unrealized. There are limitations, of course, in art and life, but in choosing to struggle with them, we become a differentiated and expanded consciousness. This power which we use to constitute our world eventually leads to unique and totally responsible beings. Awareness of these facts generates personal potency, reverence for all beings, and responsible and considerate behavior at all levels of human interaction.

In conclusion, through the spontaneous use of art materials as used in art therapy, freedom of choice is manifest. *Choice* is the key word. *Choosing is freedom in action.* The art therapist tries to give clients the largest possible range of choice that is within the realm of their physical and mental power. There is the color, the medium, the line, the form, the space, and the style. There is continuous choosing: green or red, felt markers or plasticine, thick or thin, large or small, organic or geometric, realism or abstractness.

The art product is a further example of the responsibility each of us must take as the choosing being. The finished product, as is our present state of being, is a summary of how we have used our freedom, a summary of our past choices. It is with a sense of tragedy and poignancy that we realize that the anxiety glimpsed in these acts signifies how, at a human being's core, there is a desire for competency and self-actualization. Yet it is so often allowed to be smothered with indecision and fear.

Our freedom, then, can be thought of as a pause before we leap, an interval between acts. Our leaping and acting are anxiety-producing decisions, between alternatives for which we are responsible, from which we create our uniqueness and individuality. Upon examination of these choices, we see that we always could have chosen otherwise.

Individuality

One of the most important of all acts of constituting our world is the creation of the sense of our individuality. The exploration of this act is perhaps the most important contribution of philosophy to psychotherapy. A hundred years of existential philosophy teaches that it is right and normal for each of us to seem different from other human beings. Individual consciousness is the center of all of our experience, comfortable with itself but isolated from other people, the world, and nature. The anxiety of being an individual is seen in the need to conform.

In art therapy the suppression of individuality can be seen through stereotyped imagery which comes partly from the fear of external disapproval in the use of one's own special imagery. This conformity of imagery is omnipresent with grade-school children in whom little sense of individuality exists. It is witnessed in their drawings of houses, suns, skies, and people. I do realize, as Piaget has taught, that some of this accommodation to externals in drawing is also part of children's intellectual development. On the other hand, if children were exposed more often to the spontaneous use of art, they could work through the conformity to individual expressions that would stimulate other creative and intuitive parts of the brain.

Another diagnostic measure for understanding the anxiety of individuality is seen in the lack of expression in content and color. It is as though uninhibited expression and experimentation takes an expansiveness of identity, a sense of "I Am," whereas less secure and inhibited persons cannot risk making their uniqueness known.

An example of the loss of a never-achieved sense of individuality is Jim. Jim was a 78-year-old man in my art therapy group in a convalescent hospital who was confined to a wheelchair. He had lived solely with his mother all of his life until a few years ago when she died, leaving Jim alone.

Most of Jim's conversation centered around his mother and how badly life had become for him when she passed on. Jim, to this day, had not separated from his mother. He did not draw unless I told him to. I would tell him to *draw the house you lived in for 40 years with your mother* (Figure 1.1, first house drawing) because this was something only he could draw, and I told him that no one

Figure 1.1.　The house

could see it as he could. He drew this house three different times and wanted to draw it again. As he drew each house, he was reminded that he was someone apart from his mother; he had been an individual who loved a pet, planted flowers, and had friends. Each drawing became a statement of his own existence in the reexperiencing of his past with this drawing—an "I Am."

Other ways for the art therapist to aid in bringing out a sense of the potency of individuality is by having clients draw a picture saying "No!" to someone or something they have wanted to but never dared: mother, father, husband, wife, child, or even God. This can become an angry picture. It can also be a joyful one where the person begins to see himself or herself as less of a victim and more responsible for the course of his or her life.

A simple example of our uniqueness and individuality is apparent in a group's art expressions. A quick gaze around the table at the various gestalts of color and form in the artwork is an immediate reflection of the unique and differentiated being present, no matter the level of mental health.

The most prevalent issue in psychotherapy concerns the creation of the authentic person. It is a difficult and lonely pursuit. Individuals learn that they must rely on their own resources and that suffering for their own mistakes can be an agent for change. This confrontation with isolation is anxiety-producing, but to be truly individuated means being adult, mature, and fully grown emotionally.

Birth

Another fact of human existence that comes up often in therapy is the matter of birth or rebirth. This is the anxiety that comes with disintegrations of lifestyles, relationships, and self-concepts and the emergence of new ones. To illustrate, 10 years ago John, at the age of 20, was diagnosed a schizophrenic. He was in a day treatment art therapy group with me for almost two years. He once made the statement, "I've decided to give up my career as a schizophrenic and become a regular person." This may read as a flip remark, but compared to where he had been with where he is today, this statement seems quite authentic.

John had a history of severe drug taking, a hermitlike existence of days and weeks lying isolated in bed. He used to have the appearance of a scrubby old man. In this last year of the art therapy group, he moved to a more satisfactory living arrangement and became well-groomed. He did not take drugs and voluntarily quit his prescribed medication with the approval of his doctor. He went from work as a volunteer to a paid job as a cook.

John's rebirth was a painful struggle, a struggle quite apparent in his art products and verbal associations. A review of his pictures from two years in the group showed his progress from weakly executed, fragmented lines, to geometric forms (Figure 1.2), to a more colorful imagery, to brightly colored, better-organized, and better-contained pictures (Figure 1.3). John's verbal associations, the quality of explanations, and his self-concept were all synchronous with each sequence.

The process of rebirth is visually illustrated here. His fragmented and weakly executed drawings punctuated his garbled and intellectualized, barely audible words. His amoebalike forms portrayed his floating, fantasy-filled groundless world. As the pictures gained intensity of color, his voice became louder and more certain. The black border created some containment, albeit constraints and defenses fed by his anxiety, representative of a too-early birth. His last pictures were symbols of his reaching out into the world toward the future.

There need not be one particular cause for this change in John, but there was a process occurring in his life for several years where a rerouting of old ways led to the path of health. The review of his artwork amplified this direction and served as a diary of his rebirth. The art therapist emphasized the positive and corresponding changes in life and art. Encouragement and affirmation lend support to continued recreation of the person.

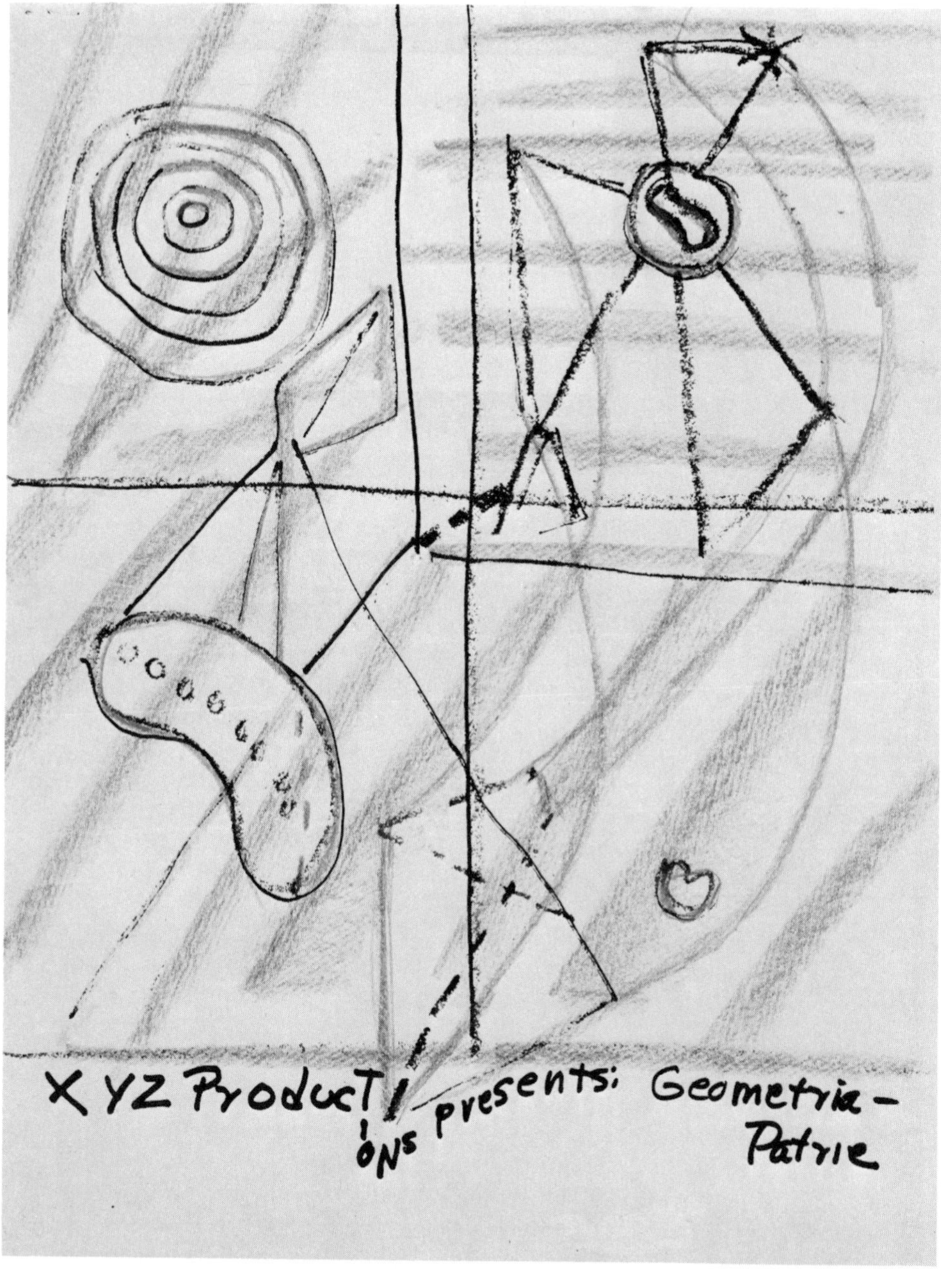

Figure 1.2.   Geometria patrie

Figure 1.3.   Flower of psychiatry

Evil

Along with issues of a person's freedom, individuality, and birth, another source of anxiety is the recognition of unredeemable evil in the world. The reality of evil in our modern world is an overwhelming fact. Just within the small arena where I work with art as a tool of therapy, evil is pervasive. Why are there rest homes or seeming "death" houses in our advanced society with its emphasis on human rights? Why are chemicals so often the alternatives for a human being's adjustment to "normalcy"? These and other "necessary" cultural evils are reflected in the individuals we all work with.

Evil is a charged word, however, and an uncomfortable one for many to deal with, one that needs attention. Each of us can find what is meaningful through examination of what is particularly evil. To illustrate this, and in response to a directive in my day treatment group to *draw what, for you, is the biggest evil in the world,* some of their pictorial answers were psychiatric hospitals, board and care homes, others making decisions for them, not liking where they lived, aging, dependencies, not feeling real, and themselves. One person responded that the blank page before starting to draw was an evil thing.

In another session, members of the group were asked to *draw how you could deal with your particular evil.* Responses were work, school, prayer, hope, to love and be loved, and to smile. What became apparent from these two sessions was that an act, a movement, some meaningful behavior on their part, was necessary to lessen their personal evil, but first they had to become aware of it and focus on it.

In the first drawing each person could see what he or she considered evil in their life and in the second drawing, their own antidote to dilute this evil. The group as a whole invested more effort than usual in executing these drawings. When clients have no focus, lack intensity, are bored, or are inattentive, they may be experiencing purposelessness and be vulnerable to evil. The art producer can help alleviate these symptoms, since the images are there in concrete form for confrontation.

This exercise reflected something in their lives that they considered evil—an evil, however, that they became conscious of and one they could do something about. They could see a way to regain some use of their freedom and could work toward a future on which many of them had given up. What is neurosis, after all, but stuckness and a lack of movement, a giving up with little pro-pulsion into the future.

Nihilism

A fifth theme of human existence is the anxiety of nihilism: life is senseless, useless; there is no truth; and faith in traditional values and morals (including

God) is unfounded. Some of the aged people I have worked with seem to be living examples of this. There is no hope. They feel they have been deserted by God, their children, and their friends. They will not draw, saying, "What's the use?" Or, if they do, they laugh and deprecate what they draw. The aged are not the only group who have retreated from the anxiety of meaninglessness in our society. The rise in drug addiction and suicide among the young is evidence that they, too, are gazing into a futureless world. Some have passed through my art therapy group in day treatment.

David, 20 years old, lost his parents when he was very young, took his first LSD trip at age 11, and attempted suicide twice. In drawing a picture of *where you would like to be,* he drew himself as a bat, which he said was "flying off into the blue." Most of his pictures had no ground; his images floated in space.

David said, "This life is hell from the day we are born and only when we die can we be freed." The people in his drawings are disembodied, inorganic, frightened creatures; portraying the ambivalence he felt about being a person. Sometimes they called for help (Figure 1.4). David had no roots; he felt homeless and alienated. His hope was for death. He believed the human condition was to be abandoned and confessed this state of mind through his artwork labeled "Dream" (Figure 1.5).

Figure 1.4.   Help

Figure 1.5.　Dream

Treatment for David focused on his available choices other than suicide. Each new picture creation served as an alternate road for his life. I pointed out to him that he himself had chosen to draw each of the available paths. He could now select one of them to follow. Working with clay was another art therapy task to help David find a sense of realness and to become more visible in the world. Again he could see, at a very basic level, how his own perceptions and conceptions gave form to the flat, amorphous, nothingness of the clay. He could see his imprint on space and time.

The therapy helped David to understand that he, and only he, could assign value to his life. It is a matter of choosing something out of nothing through either affirmation or negation. His free will and his choices, his responsibility and his subjectivity, create and uphold the values that exist for him. There is no absolute right or wrong about whatever images and forms or paths he or anyone else chooses. An important reminder here, however, is the matter of our interrelatedness. What we do always affects others. How we live is what we teach, especially to the young and the vulnerable. This fact alone can give one a sense of worth and dignity.

Death

Death is another major source of anxiety that is experienced as one of the fundamental facts of human existence. Death in our culture is coming out of its hiding place and being looked at in its proper perspective as the frame of life. Rollo May (1985) says, "Only when death was introduced into the boring drowsiness of Olympus did the home of the gods get stirred up and alive" (p. 71). Koestenbaum adds, "There are appropriate times in the life of an individual when the notion of dying can bring a greater meaning to his life" (1976, p. 2).

Our own death and the deaths of others can make clearer what it means to be human, that is, What is meaningful? What does it mean to love? What is immortality? These questions compare and can make more of an impact on a person than the biological instinctual questions of survival and procreation, psychological principles of sex and aggression, utilitarian theories of happiness, and the religious dogma of God's will. Koestenbaum claims that death helps us define human nature, and its inevitability can put us in touch with our deepest anxieties, hopes, needs, and opportunities (1976, p. 7).

The reality and inevitability of my own death became apparent to me the first time I walked into the dining hall of the convalescent hospital where the art therapy "class" was held. I had eagerly arrived with my art supplies and ideas of rejuvenation only to find a roomful of very old people sitting around the table in their wheelchairs, asleep. Each gradually awakened to my strange presence. I quickly realized that all of them had lost at least some degree of their senses—physical and mental. I was bringing to them the excitement and color of the art world, but they could neither see, hear, taste (although some have tried to eat clay and crayons), nor keep their heads or bodies erect for much, if any, involvement. This was a confrontation with a reality that I had never been exposed to. Here was one kind of summation of human life, if allowed to go on long enough.

It seemed that in their infirmity and timidity, these old people had become oblivious to their ensuing death. The word "death" was never spoken here, but complaints were never-ending. These complaints are indicative of much greater losses. Most of these old people had become infantilized and powerless and were treated as such. One 77-year-old woman asked me if I thought she had been a "good girl." For whatever reason these people had been brought to this place, they eventually abandoned their bodies to the doctors, nurses, and aides, and their minds to unconsciousness.

A way to confront death at any age is to assign value to the life already lived. Many feel they have wasted their lives. For this reason, they suffer severe grief and regret as death nears. They retire into themselves and steal away the quality of life that could be enjoyed for whatever time they have left. The art therapist

Figure 1.6.　Homes of my life

might suggest that these individuals *draw the family tree, ethnic roots, or a home in which you may have lived and loved* (Figure 1.6). This will remind them of their unique substance and value that their long life did contain most assuredly. Psychology has said that our past creates us, but philosophy adds that we can change the emotional meaning of that past (1976). Through this retroactive assigning of meaning, a person can become warm, loving, and courageous because she or he has a new found self-respect.

Another example of how to confront death with an adult of any age is to ask them to *pretend you are old and draw the most important lesson you have learned in your life.* Pictorial responses in my day treatment group were profound. The artwork symbolized the following: being responsible and trustworthy; the importance of silence and reflection; that suffering can be a learning experience; living in the present; and allowing others to give to us. The drawings became messages for everyone in the group, but particularly for the person who did the drawing. Personal values become evident through the knowledge and urgency of one's death. Again, the art process can spotlight and condense issues that arise when confronting anxiety.

With adults of all ages confrontation with their own death can come through the art and discussion of *when, where, and how you think you will die,* followed with drawings about the *feelings and thoughts surrounding that event.* Much of the fear of death is learned from society and when confronted can be found to have positive and salutary aspects. To summarize, I quote from Koestenbaum's, *The Vitality of Death:*

> In general, our response to death follows four clearly delineated stages. First, we repress the thought of our own death by projecting it onto external realities (theatre, novels, newspapers, etc.). Also, we fight with death—in war or daring acts—to prove that death cannot assail us. Second, when we recognize the reality of the *death of myself,* we experience anxiety. In fact, death, as symbol of my finitude, may well be the source of all authentic, i.e., ontological, anxiety. Third, after the anxiety of death has been faced, the anticipation of death leads to courage, integrity, and individuality. Finally, by opposing, contradicting, and fighting death, man feels his existence and achieves some of his greatest glories—in art, religion, and self-assertion. (1971, p. 26)

CONCLUDING REMARKS

In this chapter my emphasis has been on philosophy rather than the structural elements of the art process or product. Using a string of pearls as a metaphor, I look at this philosophy as the string, and the elements of art as the pearls. The ideas from this philosophical context are meant to stimulate further consideration.

The most important tool the art therapist or any other therapist brings to the client is his or her own personhood. It is the "self-made," sensitive therapist who can accept and trust his or her own sense of the client more than shorthand terms like schizophrenia. After this and beyond the art experience, the art therapist is intensely supportive and empathic toward a person's creativity and artistic expression. The art therapist's role is that of the caring other—a witness of how the client is choosing to live within the polarities of human existence. Furthermore, there is the realization that few can produce great art, but all are capable of genuine art. The consciousness that creates gives meaning to experience and emotion, not the contrary. Any ultimate meaning that is given to a finished product is that which is most true of one's experience. Rollo May (1985) says, "My firm belief is that one paints, as one writes, not out of a theory, but out of the vividness of an experience" (p. ix). The art process, as it stands by itself, is at every moment a relationship with the world and can describe human experience in the simultaneity of imagery, which would be difficult or impossible to describe in a linear, rational fashion.

⌐.I believe that the peripheral role of art in our culture is the very reason the field of art therapy was born. Responding to this, could art therapists imagine themselves with a strong philosophical background along with training in psychology and the arts? Could this teaching through the art experience have an emphasis on the person, from childhood to old age, teaching what we all need to know to make our lives more efficient, potent, and filled with joy? Or, as Yalom says, "to reacquaint the individual with something he or she has known all along" (1980, p. 16). The art therapist can be model, guide, and educator concerning the fundamental facts of human existence. This is the art therapist as philosopher.

REFERENCES

Betensky, M. (1977). The phenomenological approach to art expression and art therapy. *Art Psychotherapy*, *4*(3-4), 173–179.

Bugenthal, J. (1978). *Psychotherapy and Process*. Menlo Park, CA: Addison-Wesley Pub. Co.

Campbell, J. (1988). *The Power of Myth*. New York: Doubleday.

Koestenbaum, P. (1971). *The Vitality of Death*. Westport, CT: Greenwood.

Koestenbaum, P. (1976). *Is There An Answer to Death?* Englewood Cliffs, NJ: Prentice-Hall.

Koestenbaum, P. (1978). *The New Image of the Person*. Westport, CT: Greenwood Press, Inc.

Koestenbaum, P. (1987). *The Heart of Business*. Dallas, TX: Saybrook Publishing Co.

Laing, R. D. (1962). Ontological insecurity. In H. Ruitenbeek (Ed.), *Psychoanalysis and Existential Philosophy*. New York: E. P. Dutton.

May, R. (Ed.). (1958). *Existence*. New York: Simon & Schuster.

May, R. (1975). *Courage to Create*. New York: W. W. Norton.

May, R. (1985). *My Quest for Beauty*. Dallas, TX: Saybrook Publishing Co.

McNiff, S. (1973). A new perspective in group art therapy. *Art Psychotherapy*, *1*, 243.

Ofman, W. (1976). *Affirmation and Reality*. Western Psychological Services.

Rhyne, J. (1977). Orientations in art experience. In B. McWaters (Ed.), *Humanistic Perspectives: Current Trends in Psychology*. Monterey, CA: Brooks/Cole.

Van Den Berg, J. (1972). *A Different Existence*. Pittsburgh, PA: Duquesne University Press.

Yalom, I. D. (1980). *Existential Psychotherapy*. New York: Basic Books.

Chapter 2

Suicide as an Abortive Life Stage of Development

Julia Gentleman Byers

The relationship between suicide and art has always aroused curiosity but at the same time it fosters fear. This may be due to the powerful intention that is often apparent in a suicidal individual's art. Freud contended that slips of the tongue and/or pen or brush, misreadings of written material, forgotten instructions, bungled acts, and certain accidents can all be representations of repression. These aberrations are an effort to substitute something else for what has been repressed. Such material then contains disguised elements of the original painful memory. Freud (1901/1960) stumbled across this notion after realizing that his inability to remember the name of Signorelli was because he found it particularly unpleasant to recall that this Italian artist had committed suicide.

Maris (1981) states that one does not commit suicide when there is newness, potential for growth plus fresh starts, and a superabundance of resilience and hope. In art psychotherapy, the process of using art, which is a tangible medium for creation, can tap into the unexpressed images whose meanings reflect the internal pushes and external pulls of life.

This chapter explores the relevance of adult developmental theories to the study of suicide through an examination of the image-making process. The vignettes presented concern individuals facing life-stage transitions and/or developmental stagnation. Their "image making" may be seen as an expression syntonic to a sense of identity and self, and also of an actual concretized "image of intent" expressed in the artwork. In recognizing that "something else" can represent what is actually meant, dynamically oriented art therapy can be perceived as a working modality for the treatment of suicidal cases. The image-making process communicates what is not, nor cannot be, said or expressed in any other way.

THEORETICAL CONSIDERATIONS

Psychosexual theories of suicide see cause in the early parent/child relationships. Thus the roots of despair, in terms of early trauma, may act as hidden time fuses. R. D. Laing (1969) coined the term "ontological insecurity," specifying this as a crisis period in one's life where the sense of being alive is nonexistent. Through achieving successful psychological developmental stages within the first few years of life, the individual accumulates self-validating data of experience, making sense of the meaning in life. However, ordinary circumstances of living can threaten a person's low threshold of security. This is particularly so if his or her identity and autonomy are not completely differentiated from the original parental constellation. Szasz (1989) emphasizes the fact that certain persons who are at special risk of suicide experience a sense of ambivalence. They are, in fact, ambivalent about killing themselves and also ambivalent about not killing themselves. According to Szasz, this is not a symptom of schizophrenia; it is a symptom of being human.

A firm sense of one's own autonomous identity is required to maintain and develop relationships. Otherwise, as Laing points out, any and every relationship threatens the individual with a loss of identity. The main maneuver that some fragile personalities use to preserve identity under pressure is the maintenance of an antithesis between complete loss of "being" by absorption into another person and complete aloneness and isolation. Individual autonomy is based on the maintenance of the polarities of separateness and relatedness.

In contrast to Freudian psychosexual and Laingian phenomenological accounts, this chapter focuses on multifaceted biographies that deal with intrapersonal and interpersonal relationships that can trigger suicidal intent. These are explored from the perspective of set-points in the span of a lifetime. This corresponds with Erikson's (1964) understanding of human development, wherein the individual may make desperate attempts to reduce himself to a state of nothingness in order to reach a "rock-bottom" state. From this state it may be possible to learn new adaptational methods. Erikson hypothesized that growth stages emerge from resolutions of developmental conflicts. These include the developmental tasks of mastering *intimacy versus isolation* (youth); *generativity versus stagnation* (midlife); and *ego integrity versus despair* (older adult).

The social scientist Menninger (1968) wrote extensively as a clinician on the social implications of suicide. In part, he expanded upon the developmental aspects of Freud's concept of self-destructive behavior as symptomatic of the two instinctual drives, Eros and Thanatos. Basic polarities of young/old and destruction/creation (ages 17 to 45); masculine/feminine roles (ages 40 to 60); and attachment/separation (ages 60 to natural death) can be seen as the underlying conflictual pattern or design of a person's "life structure" at a given time.

Studies by Gouldner and Gouldner (1963) indicated that suicides tend to occur at stages in life that correspond with Erikson's developmental plateaus. The crises seem to occur at "role" transitions. People able to pass through these times of life with little trauma are better able to deal with the critical rites of passage encountered at these stressful times. Erikson (1964) and Hotchner (1966) found that the range between healthy and sick depends on the flexibility of one's body and self-image. Different types of people can tolerate and maintain the will to live at variable levels. Maris (1981), in his studies, shows that many persons who threaten suicide simply wish to transcend painful self-awareness and do not really want to die. This implies an inability to conceive of, or take on, alternative lifestyles. When an individual repeatedly fails to achieve adaptational ends, there is often extreme uncertainty and doubt as to the validity of his or her goals and means of achieving them. His or her *identity* is strongly threatened.

In a recent study of the quality of life and suicidal rates, Lester (1989) argues, based on the theory of Henry and Short (1984), that where the quality of life is better, people have less justification for blaming others for their misfortunes and so are more likely to become depressed and suicidal. In fact, Lester shows that nations and American states with a higher quality of life have higher suicidal rates, thus economic factors are not necessarily a key determinant to understanding this ontological struggle.

STAGES OF ADULT DEVELOPMENT

Young Adulthood

Zilboorg (1936) found a greater frequency of parental death (in young adulthood) in the history of those who become suicidal. Current literature supports this finding, often extending to the genogram of extended family members with the Parsons Systems Theory (Parsons, Bales, & Olds, 1955). Zilboorg stressed that there was an "ambivalent-identification" with the lost love object, suggesting an unresolved oedipal complex or transition to puberty in childhood. This leads to an inability to sustain object loss in later life as a precursor to suicide.

Midlife

In emphasizing identity role transitions as a contributing factor in suicide, Collins (1975) found that in midlife social roles multiply and become more complex. He postulates that successful personality development requires role integration and the ability to harmonize diverse, even conflicting, role expectations.

One interesting trait of social or external roles or identities is the dynamic aspect of "status," which exists independently of the individual who uses it or not. Here, the achievement of the interrelationships between work and play becomes paramount to the successful balance of an interior life and the external demands of the social and work milieu. As midlife approaches, if the transition negotiated in the separation from the family has been successful, the adult now has to deal with the changes brought about by marriage and with the management of children and a household. Changes in the quality of one's life and the intensity of competitive pressures in work, demographic relocations, and other role transitions mark a period of potential disorganization and reorganization. Depression has sometimes been labeled the subjective aspect of disorganization, which is logically necessary for reorganization for further growth.

Perhaps, as stated by Murray (1940), the ego of every adult consists of a basic "action self" plus a considerable number of "sub-selves." These are acquired through experience by such processes as introjection, identification, loving imitation, and the solution of various basic conflicts. They help the individual weather the inevitable storms of life. The key to weathering these storms successfully is whether or not the mourning of significant others is pathological or healthy. It depends on how the loss and the challenges are handled. Additionally, lifelong underlying emotional problems may emerge or be exacerbated through the loss of significant others, loss of a job, or divorce. Menninger (1938) believed that although some hopeless or depressed people do want to die, not all who see death as an "escape from pain" really want to cease living.

Late Adulthood

More marked than the earlier critical periods of identity confusion, the older adult who is prone to suicide gambles on an all or nothing attempt. The pervasive attitude, noted by Bebring (1953), is that if the individual survives, then he or she "deserves" to live. These researchers relate depressive reactions most often to a decrease or sudden deflation in a person's self-esteem. This also may occur in the loss of a job, status, or loved one. This loss of the "ideal" state of well-being, common in the earlier life patterns in a neurotic individual's development of self-esteem, is often complicated by narcissistic strivings to be a *special* person, be it saint or devil. This suggests an unusually dependent relationship on the love of others, for there is a fear of vulnerability in any loss of self-esteem.

Another issue that must be considered in the elderly is the prospect of death. Here the person perceives him or herself as a *victim*, a passive object to whom things happen that are beyond control. In actuality, the *victim* struggles with the wish to live and the need to find meaning for her or his own emotional reactions to the eventuality of death.

Busse and Pfeiffer (1973) state that when an older person attempts suicide, it is with serious intent. Should one survive, one attributes the survival to accidental factors and poor planning. This is in dramatic contrast to the frequency of the manipulative suicide attempt by the young adult.

SUICIDE AS ACTION

Suicide is addressed herein as a complicated term that emphasizes a failure of adaptation. According to Schneidman (1981), suicide encompasses a wide variety of different ranges of disturbances: dysphoria, self-abnegation, resignation, and a "terr-cum-pain" state that he calls the "biosociopsychologicoexistential state of malaise." For the purpose of definition in this chapter, suicide potential refers to the increasing lethality of the following subjective states:

1. *Suicidal ideas:* having the urge to contemplate one's own self-destruction.
2. *Suicidal threats:* overt expression either verbally or nonverbally of suicidal intent.
3. *Suicide attempts:* self-inflicted damage.

Tabachnick and Litman (1978) further relate that so-called suicidal behavior varies drastically in: the lethality of intention; degree of communication; and conscious and unconscious goals of the individuals. It also varies in cultural attitudes toward death. Often suicidal behavior is an attempt to make changes in family members—for instance, in behavior or attitudes invested in achievement, production, and success. Maris (1981) marked the term "suicidal career" to describe the history of suicidal tendencies in generational and extended family systems.

There appears to be a significant correlation between suicidal ideation, suicide threats, and suicide attempts connected to life situations that revolve around work, play, or relationship transitions, one of which varies the triggering factor, depending on the stage in life of the individual.

ART THERAPY

In clinical art therapy, the transferential elements between client and therapist may be substantially reduced or diffused through the use of the "silent partner" embodied in the artwork. Within the framework of the therapeutic relationship, the mechanism of *projection* is portrayed in the image in contrast to the therapist being the sole receiver of projections in the transference. The inclusion of the art as the silent partner facilitates the therapeutic alliance. Kreitler and Kreitler (1972), when writing on sublimation and symbolization, postulated that such concretization succeeds in giving the image a personal meaning. Through the organization of content and form in the art, messages may be contained around the core of the abstraction. Through the client's further verbal elaboration, in line with projections, recollections, and other subjectively meaningful interpretations, the therapeutic process is facilitated.

Art therapy has its own unique transferential problems, primarily that of "feeding," as expressed in the provision of art materials for consumption and production in the creation. The acceptance of the "food" (the art material) can infer a desire to go on with life and to incorporate the *good-enough* mother, in a Winnicottian sense (Winnicott, 1974). The artwork can be a substitute for the act of suicide. In the art, the patient, in the service of identity building, may recall negative childhood memories where the significant parent rejected the first self-image. There may be resistance to self-expression in reaction to this first rejection. The goal is to rebuild the *part-self* or *sub-self* that experienced rejection.

I am in agreement with Wadeson (1980) and Honig (1975), who propose that art used with a suicidal patient has other than diagnostic capabilities or the artistic rendition of the human dilemma.

The therapeutic "holding environment" of the artwork provides an opportunity to concretize the symbolic replacement of partial expression of a problem in its own perceived personal truth. The Freudian psychodynamic theories of verbal juxtapositions of saying or doing one thing and meaning another can also be seen functioning in the artwork. For example, verbal double entendres can be read into the ambivalence of transparent or translucent images; slips of the tongue can be expressed in art media accidents such as messes, or "slips" of the art materials. Also, unconsciously produced common themes in the art therapy process may contain latent messages that are important for the art therapist to be aware of.

Often, in the execution of artwork, unconscious kinesthetic energy is released to protect the flooding of psychic pain and provides some ease until the ego is stronger. If the artwork, the silent partner, can be considered to incorporate some of the qualities that Winnicott (1974) refers to as a "transitional object," it holds the power to allow the client to replay original separation and *identity building*. However, Harlow, Newcomb, and Bentler (1986) raise the question, can the person "bear to live" or "live to bear" the reexperiencing of the original pain in the separation of child from its mother which occurred at the nonverbal stage of development? Although the art can provide the catalyst for verbal exploration, the making of it is a symbiotic communion between the creator and his or her work. Thus the autonomous function of integrating parts of self may be acquired.

VIGNETTES OF ABORTED IDENTITY TRANSITIONS
IN SUICIDAL CLIENTS

The following are glimpses into the lives of individuals who expressed suicidal ideation. Through threats and attempts, these individuals sought a means of dealing with the anxiety of the changes which were occurring in the course of their adult development. These vignettes are not complete case studies. They are excerpts from the lives of those who have suffered from the phenomenon of "suicide." Exhaustive analytic interpretations, complete background material, and specific details of treatment are not provided. The overall intent is to portray the involvement and the process of image making at a crucial turning point in their existence.

THE YOUNG ADULT STAGE OF DEVELOPMENT:
INTIMACY VERSUS ISOLATION

Anne-Marie: A Hospitalized Patient

Anne-Marie, age 30, was admitted to the hospital following an unsuccessful suicide attempt with sleeping pills. This was her third admission after a diagnosis of an affective disorder. At that time, there was no history of previous suicide attempts. Her intermittent depression was treated with medication. Anne-Marie was the youngest of four brothers and one sister. Her natural father left the family when she was in her late adolescence.

Anne-Marie's records revealed that incestuous sexual abuse by her father was a major dynamic of her depressive syndrome. Until three years previously, Anne-Marie had seen her father on a regular basis. At that time she moved in with a boyfriend. Her father did not approve of the young man and withdrew from contact with his daughter. Because of Anne-Marie's ambivalence toward marriage, the boyfriend ended the relationship, and she returned to live with her mother and new stepfather.

Anne-Marie was a nurse, whose education had been funded by the father because she was very "special." She was overweight, plain but pleasant looking, and appeared younger than her 30 years. She presented herself as a withdrawn individual, who smiled but rarely spoke when she was addressed. Her mother tongue was French. Although she was fluently bilingual, in her present state she found it difficult to speak English. Her focus during art therapy was concern about her single status and that at age 30, unlike her sister, she had no family of her own.

Anne-Marie: First Session

In the first art therapy session, Anne-Marie, who seldom spoke as she drew, created two flowers, which she described as "poppies" (Figure 2.1). These two flowers, one almost hiding behind the other, appeared as she sensually smudged and stroked the pink and purple chalk pastels. This may have been expressive of her earlier relationship with her father because as she worked, she described her family before the father left home. Anne-Marie associated the poppies with opiates that "put you to sleep or take you out of this world," reflecting her suicidal attempt by drug overdose. Also the fact that her father was a war veteran lends further symbolic significance to the poppy, which represents remembrance of the dead or the loss after a battle. This is indicative of the broken home due to the divorce.

The second drawing was of a "ring that contained a horse controlled by a man, who led the horse on a rope as it went around in circles." Both were in a closed yard with a closed gate (Figure 2.2). A woman, whom she later described as her mother, sat in a rocking chair on the porch of the distant house, looking away from what was happening in the ring. This typifies the sexual abuse cases where there is anger at the mother for a lack of protection. Yet, the mother's denial of suspicious events may be repressed by the patient in an attempt to keep the good mother intact. Hendrin (1981) makes a case for depression as a

Figure 2.1.   Poppies

Figure 2.2.   Horse controlled

device to prolong the emotional ties with the parent. In this case her depression forestalls the loss of the special relationship with her father by interfering with movement to an autonomous life. The symbolism of using "sleeping pills" as the lethal weapon for her suicide attempt may be the unconscious wish to return to a lasting "sleep" with her father.

Anne-Marie: Second Session

In the second session, Anne-Marie portrayed *her family doing something.* The drawing (Figure 2.3) was of her family riding on inner tubes down icy toboggan runs. Individual members are connected to each other by ropes and by the individual paths (runs) that they follow. The gestalt formation includes a chair lift that goes around in circles. A path leading to the hilltop has footprints of the participants who have repeatedly climbed the hill. The underlying theme tends to reveal an "unsafe environment" with its sharp pine trees, spikey chair lift, and dangerous runs.

Anne-Marie: Third Session

In the third session, Anne-Marie portrays the feeling of *what it is to be alone without a controlling man* (Figure 2.4). She depicted a horse standing in the middle of a rocky stream that runs between two pointed, icy mountains. Although there are rocks in the stream that the horse can stand on, she

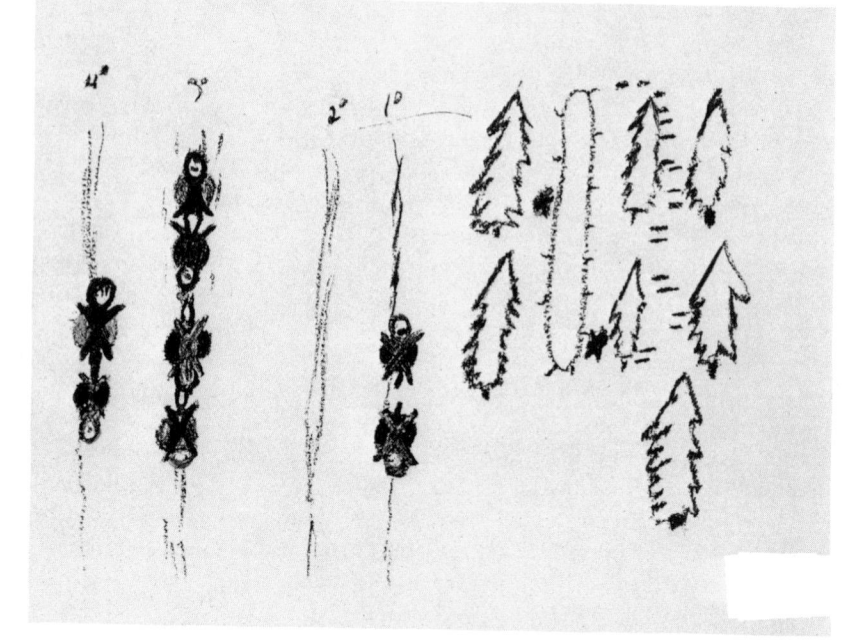

Figure 2.3.   Toboganning with the family

Figure 2.4.   Feeling alone

personifies a part of herself as the horse and as being "out of touch." She claims the stream has cooling qualities. The overall image seems to represent sexual connotations of her self-object in relation to the sexual relationship with her father. Anne-Marie declared that she needs to find another way of being "less stuck" in the stream of life and perhaps reidentify with mother.

Anne-Marie's final picture, executed the day before release, illustrates the new apartment she wishes to have (Figure 2.5). She depicts herself serving cakes while her sister operates the slide projector. On the screen she shows slides of a wind-surfing vacation while the therapist, who is seated on the couch, watches. Elements of archaic transference onto the therapist appear evident in her primitive depiction. Anne-Marie unconsciously wants to show to the mother, as transferred onto the therapist, caged feelings of the past sexual abuse "on the bed."

Other symbols drawn in the same picture of the new apartment reveal potential suicidal ideation. This is seen in the center part of her illustration which consists of a red candelabra with a fire underneath it and a cross above. To the left of the candelabra is a photo of herself, and to the right a clock that indicates the feeling of "time ticking by." The combined elements reveal an underlying association of yet another impending suicidal attempt. However, this time Anne-Marie was able to discuss it.

Figure 2.5.   Ambivalence

Through the images, she addressed her need for attention. Though the flame in the fireplace appeared large in relation to the other elements, it was contained. Anne-Marie expressed a longing to be the good little girl who is mothered. She commented that she had carried too much of a parental role in her adolescence. The rage toward both parents, regarding this collusion in the sexual abuse, had not been worked through. Therefore, Anne-Marie was unable to develop through the stage of taking on the potential future roles of wife and mother. To her, the easier choice was suicide or psychosis. The overall painting was shown to the treatment team. The consensus was that she was out of immediate danger of a suicidal attempt, although she was still at high risk.

The depiction of the black projection box could be seen as representing her inner screen of a wind-surfer in turbulent water. Unconsciously, it seemed that she was desperately attempting to keep above the water out of fear of falling into the abyss. This final primitive picture was drawn in a characteristic style reminiscent of the Québecoise culture in which she was raised. Markedly different from her previous drawings, the use of the motif of a cross in the center of the house represents the psychological state of "sealing over." The Catholic religion was extremely pervasive throughout her childhood. This consisted of ritualistically going to confession to seek redemption and be cleansed of her sins by the "good father."

As a coping mechanism her regressive behavior of returning to live with her mother reflects the desire to resolve the ambivalent feelings toward her home environment. Caught between self-destruction and the creation of a new life structure, Anne-Marie's attempted suicide was a healing effort to work through her aborted life stage. In the service of identity building, she needed to rebuild parts of herself that had experienced rejection.

Tim: A Hospitalized Patient

Tim, a 38-year-old artist, was referred to clinical art therapy while being hospitalized because of a severe depression that was compounded by suicidal thoughts. The patient, a master's level student, was in the process of completing a graduate art exhibition. He suddenly became immobilized and was unable to work on either his artwork or his thesis. This situation seriously eroded his self-confidence. He believed this was also affecting his work as a graduate teaching assistant at the university.

Tim recounted that he was a teenager in the 1960s and had been involved in the counterculture drug scene. He dropped out of school and in his late twenties moved across the country, then returned to attend art school. He became involved in a long-term relationship with a woman that ended in her tragic suicide. Prior to this, their communication and physical relationship had deteriorated. After her death, Tim chose to enter psychotherapy because of his severe somatic condition of extremely swollen joints all over his body. Over subsequent years he saw several therapists to help alleviate his symptoms of depression and a sense of alienation that periodically afflicted him. It is significant that Tim was unable to maintain any long-term therapeutic relationships, which is symptomatic of the borderline personality. As Tim stated, he "fell into" graduate school simply because he didn't know what to do next. His presenting concerns focused on feelings of hopelessness. He believed that in spite of being 38 years old, he had no marketable skills, no love life, and no immediate hope of getting married and starting a family.

Tim: First Session

Tim was extremely reluctant to draw or paint. Apologetically he finally picked up a pencil stub and executed a painstaking drawing of a tree. It was made from an accumulation of tiny marks resembling sawdust chips (Figure 2.6). Tim talked about doubting his integrity and worth as an artist. However he stated repeatedly that although it caused him physical pain, he loved doing the artwork.

Formerly as a sculptor, Tim used toxic glues and ritualistically applied them with his unprotected hands. This had resulted in serious skin and nerve-ending damage to his fingertips.

Tim listed his concerns as being loneliness, problems with sexuality, lack of a relationship, and no "real" career in his future. Developmental stagnation appeared evident in his criticism of the values of his middle-class upbringing,

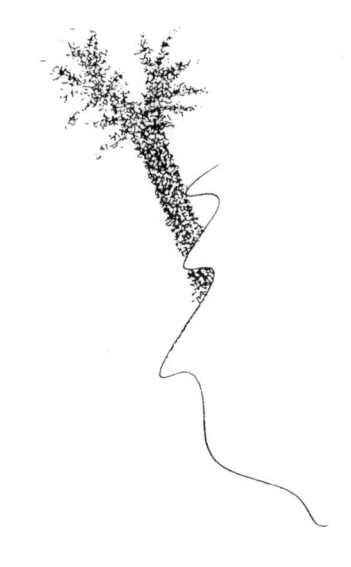

Figure 2.6.   A barren tree

while at the same time he wanted the rewards and recognition of society to "pay him" and to "lead the way." At that point he was unable or unwilling to take on the responsibilities of adulthood.

In reference to the sketch of a tree, Tim said it was a "barren tree, cut off in the middle." His associations included "being a hand that could be grasping a beached wave." Once again he voiced his inability to cope by saying, "there was not much worth living for."

Tim: Second Session

In the second session, Tim entered the room disheveled and distraught. Through repeated aggressive scribbles, he shared his anger in terms of anguish, fear, and suicidal thoughts. He said that he was discussing his recurrent suicidal ideation with friends and was rehearsing plans for such an act. Apparently no one listened to the seriousness of his intent. Tim felt guilty about having been unable to help his girlfriend through her crisis. He claimed that if he died, he would have a second chance of talking with her and could make their "relationship meaningful forever." The art therapist questioned the support system of his friends and resources. Tim explored ways of asking his friends and family to "explain" their attitudes and feelings.

Tim came from an upper class, professional, intact family. He had chosen to disengage himself from them for a period of time in his twenties. Since moving back to graduate school, he had seen them fairly often. This revealed his need to work through his unresolved relationships in the family system that precipitated his present identity crisis. Studies show that the increase in college-aged suicidal individuals may be due, in part, to the use of schoolwork as a defensive withdrawal from family and from the outside world. This adaptive function was easier for Tim's family to deal with than a child who wouldn't express any emotional feelings. Withdrawal into schoolwork was seen as "positive" behavior. In Tim's case, being "happy" paradoxically meant being free from "home." Giving up sadness, therefore, meant relinquishing the most secure part of himself, the part which he had taken from the experience of his childhood.

In this session the patient drew a pointed flamelike image which he described as "rage rushing off the page to the right, but is held back by the framed black negative space." After jabbing the paper with black chalk, Tim ended the session by compulsively rubbing the black chalk dirt off his fingers onto a new sheet of paper. This desire to rub out and erase the dirt from his hands signified the negative feelings of guilt and failure. Toward the end of the session Tim cried for the first time, stating that he was afraid to "go out there" because he feared the feeling of emptiness surrounding him. This incident represented a reliving of the separation anxiety.

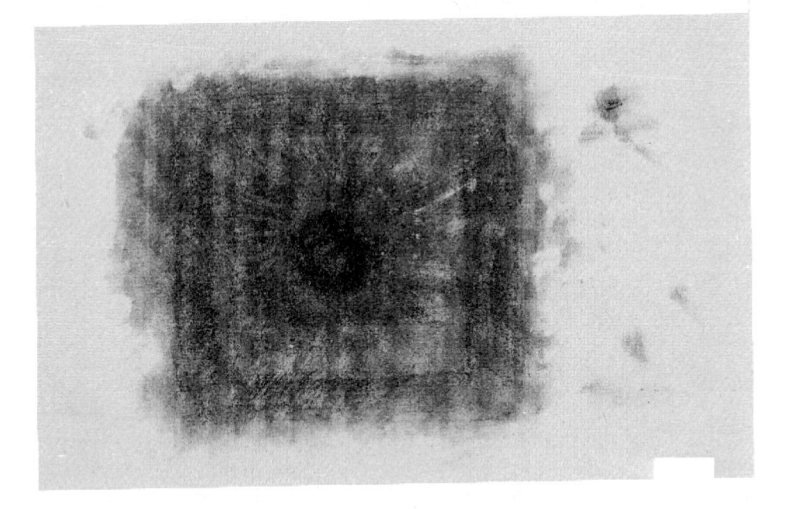

Figure 2.7.   "Entrapment" or reaching out

Tim: Third Session

Tim sketched a frame with the color purple in the center. This was followed by a sequence of extending squares in black, blue, orange, and grey. The picture depicted his sense of entrapment (Figure 2.7). Again with his dirty fingers he smudged the drawing using outward movements as he talked about what he needed to do for himself in the next few weeks. Insight was gained when he acknowledged that he expected "life" to give him what he wanted. His mother never understood his needs. As a reaction formation, Tim expected "life" to replace what he did not receive from this parent. Discussion focuses on resistance to work through unresolved family issues. He was previously unaware of the connection between his school selection and the nearby location of his family. The psychosomatic symptom of body joints swelling may have been bodily symbols of painful connections (or disconnections) in his family, where the "junctions" between members were inflamed and hurtful.

As Tabachnick and Litman (1978) proposed, Tim's suicidal ideation may have been a guilty wish for punishment, atonement, and sacrifice to make restitution. His self-destructive use of his art materials bears this out. In his work as a professional artist, he permanently damaged his fingertips by his misuse of corrosive glues. The dream of creating a "normal" family with his girlfriend was dramatically aborted. Similar to the clients in the studies by Gouldner and Gouldner (1963), who claim that the inability to sustain a role transition often precipitates suicidal action, Tim was unable to cope with life. In addition, he was creatively blocked, which could be seen as a form of "suicidal" behavior on the part of an artist in graduate school. At discharge, Tim was able to recognize his destructive tendencies and joined an art gallery group of artists who meet once a week to discuss their work. The group served as a socializing agent for Tim, and it also helped him to discontinue his self-inflictions.

Jack: An Outpatient

In an outpatient setting, Jack, a youthful, balding 42-year-old man, was referred to clinical art therapy because of suicidal ideation and depression. These symptoms followed the birth of his first son. He began to have difficulties maintaining his role as an insurance broker and a husband. The first three months of treatment were relatively uneventful and focused on his coping with his work, plus relationships with family and friends. Jack consistently drew spontaneously while verbally describing current stories and events that were happening in his life. He had difficulty correlating what he had said with what he had drawn. When the art therapist informed Jack that the therapy must cease within the next two months because she was moving away, Jack became enraged. The repressed feelings toward his father's suicide were suddenly exposed.

Jack: A Significant Session

In this session, Jack began drawing a newspaper with lines instead of headlines and text. He related this to his dislike of reading the newspaper early in the day. He drew several versions of this feeling, commenting on how it annoyed his wife that he "wasn't more with it." Since a therapeutic alliance had been developed, the therapist asked Jack to *relate the news that could be read into his drawing.* He then made a heavy cloud and beneath it he sketched himself growing out of the ear of another person (Figure 2.8). Almost in a trancelike state, Jack recounted that his father, who was a town mayor, had committed suicide. He was 12 years old at the time and read about it in the newspaper headlines. Jack was told to stay with a neighbor while funeral arrangements were made. His grieving mother neither comforted him nor explained what happened. After the traumatic event, Jack and his mother moved to another city to avoid the embarrassment and shame. He was told not to tell the truth of his father's death to anyone. This message was so deeply implanted that the facts of his father's death eluded even Jack himself. The child felt completely abandoned and over the next few years his mother became more and more detached.

As an acting-out adolescent, he was hospitalized for his uncontrollable behavior. The patient had felt guilty about being unable to replace his father for the sake of his mother. He was in desperate need of a male role model throughout his youth. Jack commented that his drawing represented the fact that his identity grew from "what I heard about my father rather than having a real father," and that he still felt bitter and remorseful. Because he was the same age his father was when he had committed suicide by hanging, Jack said he could now make "sense of the current nightmares of being choked." However, Jack feared that he was ill-equipped to father his own child since he lacked a role model.

Figure 2.8. "What was heard and grew"

The transferential issues in the art therapist's leaving and Jack's drawing recurrent "images" of himself served to uncover an illusion of self, syntonic to reexperiencing the childhood trauma as a working-through process.

Jack: Termination Sessions

Throughout the last sessions, Jack focused on his newly born son. He stated "in my son, I have the potential to find the good parts of myself." These were aspects that he did not receive from his own father. In the last session he drew himself holding hands with his growing son (Figure 2.9). The transferential drawing could also represent his reluctance to end therapy. The child may symbolize himself "holding hands with the therapist." The heavily drawn interior of the body shapes suggests that he still yearned to be protected and cared for.

The stressful demands of parenthood in the early childrearing years resurfaced in aggressive feelings which had not been dealt with effectively in his own psychological development. The appropriate timing of his aggressive release, contained within the therapeutic holding environment, provided Jack with an alternative to "suicide as action": He was therefore able to stop the pattern of "suicidal career" in his own family system.

OLDER ADULT STAGE OF DEVELOPMENT: INTEGRITY VERSUS DESPAIR

Reg: A Hospitalized Patient

Reg, a 69-year-old man who owned and drove his own taxicab, lived by himself in a fashionable downtown apartment. His threat of suicide was viewed as a means of taking refuge in the hospital. Because of his brief hospitalization, family background information was limited. Reg had been married for a short time. He had not remarried in the 26 years since his divorce and had lost touch with his large family of 11 siblings. He left home at age 16 to join the army. He described himself as a "kind of nomad" after having completed grade school. Events that precipitated his admission were in part due to his recurring impotence. This situation had caused his girlfriend, a prostitute and drug user, to abandon him. Reg suddenly stopped drinking alcohol and smoking after 46 years of serious abuse. He became increasingly socially isolated and lacked the relationships provided by the other substance abusers. It was his repeated urge to jump from the seventh floor of his apartment building that led him to the emergency ward of the hospital.

Reg: First Session

Reg was seen four times in art therapy. In the first session, he painted carefully and slowly. A tree picture was described as an "empty" body figure and

Figure 2.9.   Holding hands with son

a "barren" tree (Figure 2.10). The "empty" body form was devoid of any definition of inner body parts, genitals, or legs. It appeared as an open cavity which the adjacent phallic tree could fill. It seemed to be a dismembered, exaggerated phallic body part. Reg commented that there were no "descendents" to carry on his name. He referred to his relationships with women as "nomadic" since they were usually prostitutes. Reg shrugged his shoulders unknowingly in response to the numbers he painted above the tree and figure. His attempt to restructure and make sense of his depression was apparent. Repeated themes of "three" in subsequent pictures may indicate early unresolved oedipal conflicts.

In his second picture, Reg painted red cars on a road going nowhere. Parts of the construction resembled a childhood "hang-man" configuration game. Fear of social desolation appeared to be his predominant concern. Most of his relationships had been paid for. Prostitutes and alcohol furnished him with sex, companionship, and sedation. Even his profession of taxi driver relegated his contacts with others to a "paid" type of human encounter. His dependency on alcohol had tended to seal over the pain of separation and loss associated with the early stages of object loss. Reg drew several bottles, recounting "some good times," but felt he should now find another way of relaxing; to be in a better state of mind in case "something happened." The final drawing portrayed a clock, indicating that "time was running out." The artwork also contained a cold, dead blue sun that represented the underlying emotional deprivation and lack of a wish to go on.

Reg: Second Session

In the next session Reg drew an empty church with stairs leading to it. It had no doors or windows. A ladder "leading nowhere" was included, and an unidentified leaflike form. Paralleling the "adult stage of integrity versus despair," the transition between midlife to older adulthood includes coming to terms with the meaning of life and one's involvement with it. Reg was depressed and remorseful. He believed he had "sinned" and that there was "no way out, with no redemption for him."

Reg: Fourth Session

In the fourth session, an image of the bottle reemerged. Surgical scissors drawn in the same picture appear indicative of unresolved castration anxiety related to his apparent impotence. Reg worried that "something inside wasn't right." Subsequent paintings of games, a checkerboard, and a baseball diamond portrayed a "win or lose" attitude, as if life was a game in which you gambled "all or nothing." While he drew, Reg revealed that he had stashed away a substantial amount of money in his apartment. His financial assets represented his worth and an ability to save and use money to fulfill his fantasy. He had wanted to retire to the South Seas with the girl of his dreams, his former prostitute girlfriend. Reg had told her about his money before he learned of her involve-

Figure 2.10.　Empty body, barren tree

ment with drugs. His near suicidal attempt was a way for him to escape from a situation wherein he feared he would "lose all" if his girlfriend stole his money. If his money was gone, he believed he would have severe difficulty in making sense of his life. The diamond baseball field drawn in a phallic configuration was again repetitive of the triangular relationships in unresolved oedipal issues. Reg was offered the opportunity to continue in outpatient therapy. The treatment goal was to find alternative choices and ways of dealing with immediate socialization and environmental issues.

As found in studies by Resnik and Cantor (1970) of suicidal roles in older adults, feelings of helplessness and hopelessness about the possibility of change and status added to Reg's feelings of inadequacy. He perceived of himself as a victim. As Schneidman (in Maris, 1981) points out, in suicidal cases, the key to functioning, to wisdom, and to life itself is often to choose the least unpleasant alternative that is practical and attainable. Reg was able to give up the alcohol which had a major effect on his life. He became a "reformed" alcoholic and joined a chess association which met regularly for tournaments and to exchange crossword puzzles. This form of sublimation served to "outwit" his opponents for endless hours.

Roger: Outpatient

Roger, 63 years old, was seen in art therapy following hospitalization for an apparent suicide attempt. Roger suffered from cirrhosis of the liver caused by years of alcohol abuse. He had recently undergone surgery for the insertion of a shunt to release water retention. Prognosis was that he only had six months to live. Since his operation, he had been on a special low salt diet and had to measure out all food in grams. Roger had become compulsive about following the diet, convinced that if he deviated minimally it would kill him. Several times he phoned the hospital emergency room in a panic because he had eaten a pickle and believed it fatal. The salt-laden pickle presented an almost lethal temptation when he felt out of control. Roger stated that the "bad little boy" inside him made him swallow poison, the severe dosage of salt content, that was indeed lethal for his body, and attempt suicide.

Roger had been married previously. His present wife was 20 years his junior and they did not have children. He had been a highly qualified electronics technician who had not worked in his field for years. He had lost several well-paying jobs because of his alcohol problem. Roger was an avid and talented musician and had always supplemented his income by playing piano in bars. He continued to do this intermittently after losing his last full-time job. His wife, who worked in an office, was able to support the two of them.

Roger: First Session

Roger presented himself as a bright, articulate, intelligent man who appeared to "talk" through his drawings as he created them. He began making a dark cloud over his head that expressed feelings of "guilt and bad luck" that he carried around with him from his youth (Figure 2.11). Roger's mother was Jewish and his father was Catholic. Although he was raised Catholic, his mother never converted. This led to problems of religious identification that caused anxiety from an early age. He felt closely aligned with his mother's faith. As he was very attached to his mother, Roger was the only sibling to remain in the same city with her until her death. His brother and married sister did not have the same problems of identification as they were attached to the Catholic Church.

Through the art, Roger pointed out his fears of being out of control. He portrayed hurting himself with a knife that he is holding to his throat and also injuring his wife with that weapon. The picture also included the sketch of himself as a child out of control, spewing black things out. In the center of the paper, he expressed his magical thinking through sunglasses as a metaphor to avoid seeing the mirror reflections of the depth of his own despair. Roger refused to go anywhere without his sunglasses because otherwise "people would see the bad inside him." By constantly wearing the glasses, he felt he could function almost normally in the "real world."

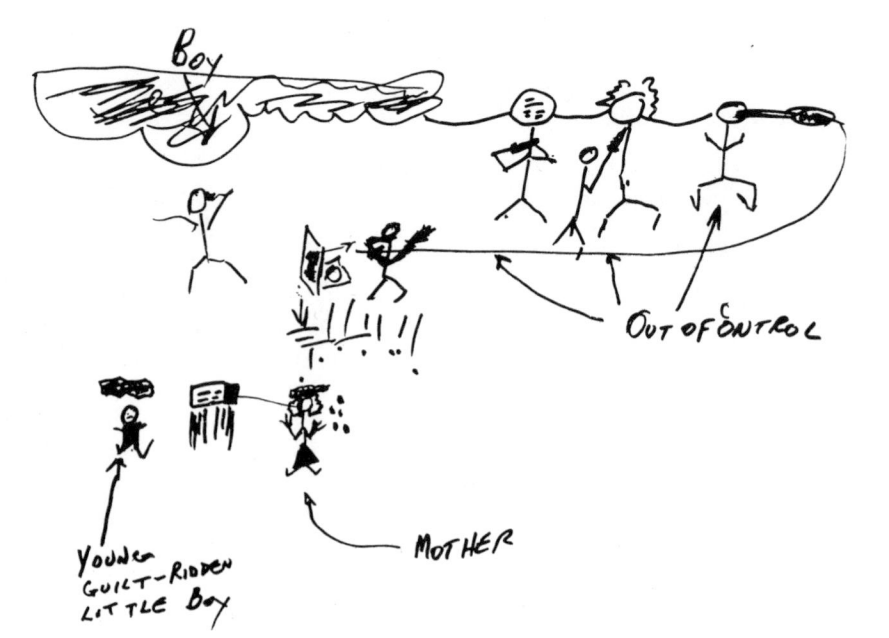

Figure 2.11.   Guilt-ridden little boy

Roger: Three Sessions Later

While engaged in a life review, Roger depicted his fears of being too far from home. He had placed himself in the middle of the paper, wobbly-legged and trapped, at the "point of no return" between "somewhere" and home. He remembered an incident when his mother left him for a short time while he was sitting in a church grotto. He did not understand why she had left him alone. The experience was a frightening memory of being lost and abandoned. This recall may have been a warning that remembering too much, even through the symbolic, was too painful. He appeared to be struggling to find the "home" inside himself where he didn't feel so empty.

Roger: Several Sessions Later

In another session, Roger was directed to *draw what he was currently feeling*. He drew himself and his wife in bed, expressing some of his sexual frustrations and impotence. He illustrated a raging child within who said "let me out, I'm gonna kill you and everybody." He then drew his "censor" or his outside person who knew the difference between right and wrong, but most often did wrongly. In the same picture, he attempted to combine the guilt ridden little boy (the id) and the "censor" (the superego), into a "we" (the ego). The composite configuration he created was labeled "I-Two" and shows an ambiguous mouth. The body of this new childlike figure is empty in the belief that he lacked substance. This may represent the place where his fluid, bloated body held the shunt that was necessary to empty out his excess water.

Roger: Twelfth Session

Toward the end of his 12 sessions, Roger reviewed his unfinished business in a drawing that the therapist had encouraged. It was created in a linear schema, beginning with his enclosed house, from where he often walked to a local park (Figure 2.12). The path he would take zigzagged and at the end was a stick figure of himself holding a knife, contemplating suicide, while his wife had called the police because he was late coming home. The underlying images of the cross on the mountain, time running out, and candles burning expressed despair about his life coming to an end. Since he had about six months to live he was beginning to understand his suicidal attempts as a way to escape his bodily deterioration. Other issues that emerged through the artwork included his failure as husband and provider. According to Roger, "these things traditionally defined him as a man." His identity and his life were in crisis. Roger was finally able to discuss the problems that were linked with his wife and his concerns about death. His fears of being lost and empty were tied into the conflict about which church or belief would "take care of him." He had rejected the Catholic Church in his youth, and now he was unsure of Judaism since he was accepted only because of his mother's faith.

Roger: Last Session

In his last session, Roger illustrated his way of trying to cope with what he had accepted as his short future. He recalled his love of music and how he conscientiously taught himself to play because he could not afford lessons. He practiced from a book of exercises which were to be completed in 60 minutes, until he could do them perfectly. Roger recounted the time that he became enraged at a friend to whom he had lent some precious music. In frustration, his friend tore up the music and "disembowelled the piano, leaving only a skeleton." The piano was synonymous with himself, as a victim of circumstance. He also regretted "not trying harder," allowing the "enraged child within" to take over, and the horrible loss of a loved object (his mother) still trying to control his life and death.

Near the end of the session, he drew and spoke of what he wanted said at his eulogy: "I paid my own way." Looking at the therapist he said, "that's the Jewish way, you know." The art was drawn with a blue felt pen, revealing his sadness and reflecting his early emotional deprivation. By playing the piano again, he could create a harmony, or create melodies to express his life. Whether these melodies would take the form of the Catholic mass or the chanting of the Jewish mourning rites of "Shiva" was still unresolved.

Figure 2.12.   Unfinished business

The return to musical structure seemed to be an attempt to restructure and integrate positive and negative attributes of his personality. This corresponds to the stages of dying that one goes through as described by Kubler-Ross (1969). Roger was beginning to mourn and accept death rather than "abort" what precious time he had left. Perhaps his bloated stomach, which had to be emptied periodically, symbolically represented the "child" inside, one whose entry to the world was never resolved. His dependency on alcohol had served as a self-feeding oral substitute for the nurturing mothering relationship that he never had. As death approached, Roger was still trying to resolve the lack of belonging to a symbolic spiritual family.

The attachment/separation stage underlined Roger's life structure and typifies Erikson's stage of ego integrity versus despair. The apparent suicide attempt as an abortive life stage was an attempt to escape from physical pain and mental trauma.

DISCUSSION

Each of the vignettes shows what Winnicott (1974) terms the "impingement of reality." Here the individual experiences full terror when he or she senses that this world is liable, that at any moment it could crash in and obliterate all identity. The symbolic lethality of the suicidal gesture, or attempt, reflects a sense of the anxiety that becomes unbearable.

Anne-Marie, through the abuse of sleeping pills, presented her sense of being swallowed up by her relationship with her father, meanwhile lacking the protection of the mother. The possibility of a new identity through marriage and motherhood challenged her present fragile autonomy. This would put her attempt into the aborted developmental stage of intimacy versus isolation.

Tim expressed his dread of being stifled in relationships and being unable to communicate. This was symbolized through his compulsion to torture himself with the misuse of glues. The ritualized use of glue itself may be synonymous with the "stickiness" of encounters in relationships. He was unable to make the role adjustments to a new family life. Developmentally, he fitted into the crisis in Erikson's generativity versus stagnation stage.

Reg imagined jumping off the seventh floor to allow the weightlessness of air to engulf him, perhaps to hurl himself into the void. This may be symbolic of his empty feeling following the death of his mother. The association of a phallic building represented his fear of impotence and his male identity. The dynamic of his status in life was rocked, revealing his psychological fragility. In Erikson's model, Reg was halted in the generativity versus stagnation phase.

Jack's recurrent nightmares of being choked came with the birth of his son, as well as his chronological age, which matched the age at which his father committed suicide. In his new role as father, Jack feared that he was ill-equipped to face the challenges of parenthood, since the child within himself was needy.

Potential identification with his father's mechanism of aborting career pressures through suicide threatened his identity and autonomy. This correlates with the aborted stage of ego integrity versus despair.

Roger, in a symbolic sense of being drowned by the tears shed for the loss of his mother, literally flooded himself with toxins, seriously affecting his bodily condition. Physical deterioration took over his sense of integrity and self-worth. Finally, in terms of the model of adult developmental theory being used, the stage transition of ego integrity versus despair was being aborted.

Finding a way to orchestrate the appropriate timing and release of aggression in constructive self-assertion is one of the major problems in the therapy of depression. The frame, or the therapeutic holding of the image, lends itself to the full expression of the conflict. This, together with the concretized recorded artwork, functions as a statement of the changes individuals undergo in the long-term therapeutic process.

If there is a right to kill oneself, perhaps it is limited by the ability to understand the meaning and consequences of death, both to one's self and others who are significant. Signorelli's suicide inadvertently ushered in a new way of understanding certain human acts through Freud's interruption of symbols. These early warning signs can be seen as messages to prevent the individual from acting out his or her meaning in the ultimate finality of death.

CONCLUDING REMARKS

The vignettes in this chapter portray how the art therapy process taps into the symbolic meaning of the individual's suicidal ideas, threats, or attempts. The goal of the short-term hospitalized treatment cases is to create a tangible support activity so that the suicidal individuals have time to reconsider the meaning of their lives. More adaptive ways of living are found as a means of working through each patient's "transitional" crisis. In long-term cases, a deeper analytic understanding of the balance between the clients' aggressive and libidinal drives and their operational defense system is explored. Corresponding to Erikson's (1964) understanding of adult human development and other psychosocial theories, examples of the hospitalized and outpatients at young, middle, and older adulthood illustrate how each individual gained awareness of the meaning of his or her action as an abortive life stage of development. The symbol of each person's means to attempt suicide underlines the psychological complexities of their ontological crisis. Art therapy can reveal the inner images and potentially decode these associations with this critical experience, thus transforming destructive behavior into new hope.

REFERENCES

Bebring, E. (1953). The mechanisms of depression. In P. Greenacre (Ed.), *Affective Disorders*. New York: International Universities Press.

Busse, E., & Pfeiffer, E. (1973). Mental illness in later life. *Annual Review of Psychology American Psychiatric Association Report*. Washington, DC: American Psychiatric Press.

Collins, R. (1975). *Conflict Sociology: Toward an Exploratory Science*. San Diego: Academic Press.

Erikson, E. (1964). *Childhood and Society*. New York: Norton.

Freud, S. (1901/1960). *Psychotherapy of Everyday Life*. London: Hogarth Press.

Gouldner, A. W., & Gouldner, H. P. (1963). *Modern Sociology*. New York: Harcourt, Brace & World.

Harlow, L., Newcomb, M., & Bentler, P. M. (1986). Depression, self-derogation, substance use and suicidal ideation: Lack of purpose in life as a meditational factor. *Journal of Clinical Psychology, 42,* 5–21.

Hendrin, H. (1981). Psychotherapy and suicide. *American Journal of Psychotherapy, 2,* 77–85.

Henry, A. F., & Short, J. F., (1954). Suicide and Homicide. New York: Free Press.

Honig, S. (1975). Ideation of the artwork of suicidal patients. *Art Psychotherapy, 2,* 77–85.

Hotchner, A. E. (1966). *Papa Hemingway*. New York: Random House.

Kreitler, M., & Kreitler, S. (1972). *Psychology of the Arts*. Durham, N.C.: Duke University Press.

Kubler-Ross, E. (1969). *On Death and Dying*. New York: MacMillan.

Laing, R. D. (1969). *The Divided Self*. New York: Penguin Books.

Lester, D. (1989). The quality of life and suicide rates in american cities in the 1930's. *Psychological Reports, 65,* 1358.

Maris, R. W. (1981). *Pathways to Suicide: A Survey of Self-Destructive Behaviors*. Baltimore, MD: Johns Hopkins University Press.

Menniger, K. A. (1938). *Man Against Himself*. New York: Harcourt Brace.

Menniger, K. (1968). *Crime of Punishment*. New York: Viking.

Murray, H. A. (1940). Dead to the world: The passions of Herman Melville. In E. S. Schneidman (Ed.), *Essays in Self-Destruction*. New York: Science House.

Parsons, T., Bales, R. F., & Olds, J. (1955). *Family Socialization and Interaction Process*. Glencoe, Illinois: Free Press.

Resnik, H. L., & Cantor, J. M. (1970). Suicide and aging. *Journal of American Geriatric Society, 18,* 152–158.

Schneidman, E. S. (1981). In R. W. Maris (Ed.), *Pathways to Suicide: A Survey of Self-Destructive Behaviors*. Baltimore, MD: Johns Hopkins University Press.

Szasz, T. (1989). Suicide and psychiatric coercion. *The Journal of Humanistic Psychology, 29*(3), 383.

Tabachnick, N., & Litman, R. (1978). Suicide Prevention Center, Los Angeles, unpublished paper.

Wadeson, H. (1980). Suicide expressions in images. *American Journal of Art Therapy, 14,* 75–87.

Winnicott, D. W. (1974). *Playing and Reality*. Middlesex, England: Penguin Books.

Zilboorg, G. (1936). Differential diagnostic types of suicide. *Archeology, Neurology, Psychiatry, 35,* 270–291.

Chapter 3

Treatment of Women with Eating Disorders

Darcy Lubbers

Anorexia nervosa and bulimia nervosa, previously considered rare disorders, now constitute a widespread and serious problem among adolescent and young adult women in this country. The reported incidence of these disorders has risen dramatically over the last two decades. Statistics show that 90 to 95 percent of the individuals affected are female. They are disproportionately white and largely come from middle- and upper-middle-class backgrounds (Herzog & Copeland, 1986). The 5 to 10 percent of reported cases in males present a clinical picture that is different from the females; usually there is a greater degree of psychopathology present, along with a less favorable treatment prognosis (Brumberg, 1988).

Anorexia nervosa and bulimia nervosa have become "in" diseases among well-to-do young women, particularly in environments such as college campuses, where strong elements of peer influence exist. In these settings, estimates of females with these disorders run as high as 20 percent (Herzog & Copeland, 1986; Striegel-Moore, 1989). This epidemic appears to be largely confined to the United States and other westernized societies such as western Europe and Japan.

These illnesses form complex, multifaceted, and multidetermined clinical pictures, with impinging cultural, familial, intrapsychic, interpersonal, and physiological factors. They are conditions characterized by the relentless pursuit of a thin body size, and once established, each syndrome acquires autonomous characteristics and a life of its own. Each is associated with an exaggerated fear of weight gain, and fat, often to delusional proportions, which becomes the focus of the individual's life. An attempt is made to solve psychological issues or conflicts through the concrete manipulation of intake and body shape (Bruch, 1973; Crisp, 1980; Garfinkel & Garner, 1982; Sours, 1980).This is at the cost of other physical and psychological aspects, and in spite of the syndromes' life-threatening consequences. Physically, anorectics may suffer from amenorrhea, elevated growth hormone, osteoporosis, abnormal body temperature, cardiac arrhythmia, and anemia. Because of the vomiting and purging rituals, bulimics may suffer from Ipecac poisoning, gastric rupture, esophagitis, electrolyte imbalances, dehydration, swelling of the parotid glands, and erosion of dental enamel, due to the excessive acids brought up in vomiting.

Although eating disorders are usually described in the literature as separate disorders, they may be viewed as spectrum illnesses. Victims of the two disorders share many of the same concerns and behaviors regarding their intense fear of fat. In 1980, the DSM-III listed anorexia nervosa and bulimia as separate disorders; in 1987, the DSM-III-R listed anorexia nervosa and bulimia nervosa as separate but related disorders, while subtyping another category of bulimics who display bingeing and purging behaviors, but who also manifest symptoms of anorexia nervosa. In both types of patients, thinness is believed to be the magical solution to life's problems. Both types of individuals share tendencies towards denial of feelings, a mechanistic view of the body, and strivings towards outward perfection and success. Anorectics, who are at one end of the spectrum, attempt to control their bodies by severe restriction of food intake, whereas bulimics, at the other end of the spectrum, try to manage by compulsive binge-eating, and then purging through self-induced vomiting, laxative abuse, or diuretics. However, a crossover of symptomatology is not unusual. For example, episodes of alternate bingeing and fasting occur for some anorectics (these are given the label of "bulimic anorectics"), while occasional periods of fasting interspersed with the binge and purge cycles also happen with some bulimics.

CLINICAL ART THERAPY TREATMENT

The artwork of patients with anorexia nervosa has been referred to as a notable phenomenon (Bruch, 1978; Crisp, 1980). However, very little has been written to date on the subject of clinical art therapy with either anorectics or bulimics. Mitchell (1980) and Bruch (1978) view artwork as a valuable tool for anorexic patients to gain self-awareness. Crowl (1980) presents examples of the anorectic's art as being related to three areas of conflict: self-image, self-esteem, and control. Haeseler (1982) ties in the successful use of art therapy with Kohut's (1971) work in the area of narcissistic disorders. Haeseler postulates that the patient is able to utilize the art therapist as a self-object. Wolf, Willmuth, Gazda, and Watkins (1985) present examples of anorexic, inpatient artwork, which accompany an analysis of issues, conflicts, defense mechanisms, and the utilization of the art as a bridge to other treatment modalities. Ticen (1990) explores the relationship of bulimia nervosa and the history of sexual abuse in some patients.

Creating a trusting alliance is often extremely difficult with eating-disordered patients because of their strong resistence to treatment. They view their illness as ego-syntonic and mistrust those who may "take it away from them." The art psychotherapist has an advantage in developing a trusting relationship due to the nonthreatening nature of the art process. It removes the constant pressure for patients to talk about themselves. The immediate, enjoyable art experiences foster feelings of trust and positive relating, which are necessary before important therapeutic work can begin.

A paralyzing sense of personal ineffectiveness is a commonly observed trait of eating-disordered clients. They are convinced that they are inadequate, inferior, and despised by others. All of their efforts are directed toward hiding these fundamental flaws by being "perfect" dieters and having "perfect" bodies. Successful psychotherapy for anorectics and bulimics is oriented more towards the patient's establishing a sense of trust in her own feelings and abilities than it is towards the more traditional psychodynamic concepts of insight.

For these women, conflicts concerning control and autonomy have been acted out compulsively and obsessionally in the arena of food. It is therefore critical that they learn how to refocus their energies in adaptive, healthy ways, with the goals of achieving autonomy and gaining control over their lives.

Art therapy gives these patients a way to gain a sense of mastery and achievement through task completion and to learn new skills through the manipulation of the media. The creation of the art product affords them renewed energy and potentials for positive self-expansion. Interpersonal skills are improved by practicing and visualizing behaviors, along with role-playing techniques.

Milieu Treatment Approach

An inpatient program for treating anorexic and bulimic adult patients will ideally be both intensive and highly structured, yet at the same time, supportive, nonpunitive, and humanistic in its philosophy. The program must be designed to encourage the eating-disordered patient to confront her illness and to facilitate "giving up" the eating disorder in exchange for a more adaptive, healthy lifestyle. To accomplish this, the program needs to offer a variety of treatment strategies built around a specially trained, multidisciplinary treatment team. The team, under the supervision of the clinical director, should include the patient's admitting doctor, clinical art therapist, primary nurse, dietician, and possibly other adjunctive therapists. The multidisciplinary approach promotes uniformity and consistency in treatment, while minimizing opportunities for manipulativeness and splitting by the patient. The functions of the treatment team are as follows: (a) a comprehensive assessment of each patient upon admission, (b) the formulation of a multiaxial analysis; (c) delineation of effective treatment strategies, (d) production and communication of goals, and (e) the enlistment of the patient's alliance for therapeutic purposes.

Formulation of each individual therapy plan includes evaluations of the degree to which each of the following factors are present: (a) drive for thinness; (b) bulimic episodes; (c) body dissatisfaction; (d) sense of personal ineffectiveness/ lack of self-esteem; (e) perfectionism; (f) interpersonal distrust; (g) difficulties with interoceptive awareness of bodily sensations; and (h) maturity fears.

Because of the complexity of the eating disorder symptomatology, the mulitfactor orientation must prevail as an underlying approach to treatment. Changes must be accomplished in several areas: improvement of abnormal nutrition, issues of control, clarification of maladaptive patterns of family interaction, and correction of erroneous assumptions that form the basis of self-deceptive and life-threatening "pseudosolutions."

This chapter delineates the role of clinical art therapy within the milieu, team approach. It addresses specific areas in the treatment of eating-disordered women including assessment, body image, ventilation of feelings, family dynamic issues, issues of control, cognitive distortions, enhancement of self-esteem and personal effectiveness, and individuation. The chapter also addresses the advantages inherent in this modality for dealing with these issues. Examples of patient artwork illustrate the issues as they are manifested and portray the specific techniques that are utilized. The following section of this chapter focuses on the art therapy for anorectics, and the section after that on the treatment of bulimics. The complexity of the dynamics involved for both types of eating-disordered patients are addressed herein, as well as the similarities and differences of their presentation. A section on specific group art therapy techniques is also included.

ANOREXIA NERVOSA: DIAGNOSTIC CRITERIA

The *Diagnostic and Statistical Manual of Mental Disorders,* or *DSM-III-R* (American Psychiatric Association, 1987), contains descriptions of diagnostic categories of all recognized mental disorders. The four diagnostic criteria cited for anorexia nervosa are:

A. Refusal to maintain body weight over a minimal normal weight for age and height, e.g., weight loss leading to maintenance of body weight 15% below that expected; or failure to make expected weight gain during period of growth, leading to body weight 15% below that expected.

B. Intense fear of gaining weight or becoming fat, even though underweight.

C. Disturbance in the way in which one's body weight, size, or shape is experienced, e.g., the person claims to "feel fat" even when emaciated, believes that one area of the body is "too fat" even when obviously underweight.

D. In females, absence of at least three consecutive menstrual cycles when otherwise expected to occur (primary or secondary amenorrhea). (A woman is considered to have amenorrhea if her periods occur only following hormone, e.g., estrogen, administration). (p. 67)*

*Reprinted with permission from The American Psychiatric Association.

ART PSYCHOTHERAPY WITH THE ANORECTIC

Assessment

The process, form, content, color, and associations to the artwork reflect information about personality development, personality traits, and unconscious behaviors. In addition, House-Tree-Person (Buck, 1974) and Family (Burns & Kaufman, 1972) drawings that are created from the beginning of treatment to the end are useful assessment instruments.

For the House-Tree-Person test, the patient is told to *make two separate drawings—one with a lead pencil and one with colored markers—of a house, a tree, and a person.* The penciled images frequently indicate the patient's defense mechanisms, while the other reflects the underlying dynamics.

The House-Tree-Person assessment drawing done by Amy, a 24-year-old woman, is typical of initial drawings done by anorectic patients at the beginning of treatment (Figure 3.1). In this case, the patient chose to use her own paper, which was considerably smaller than the paper offered to her. She also disregarded the instructions by choosing to put both images on the same sheet of paper. Amy thereby passively initiated a control struggle with the therapist and limited her symbolic field of nurturance by denying herself additional art materials. The patient's imagery uses very little of the space on the page, and the penciled sketch is nearly invisible. All of these factors typify the anorectic's extremely low self-esteem and sense of nonexistence.

As the family dynamics are often represented in the house drawing, it is striking to note that the image on the right side of Figure 3.1 is entirely filled in black. When this was mentioned by the therapist, the patient spontaneously verbalized her associations that living at home with her family was very depressing and filled with conflict.

Figure 3.1.   House-tree-person assessment drawing

Suzanne, age 39, also made a House-Tree-Person assessment drawing when she began treatment. She was extremely hesitant about using the art materials and completed only the first half of the directive by making a pencil drawing. The patient was concerned that her drawing was not "good enough."

Like Amy, Suzanne used very little of the space on the page, and the line quality was extremely light. The images included only a bare minimum of detail. The house lacked the essential elements of doorway and windows, and the tree was stark and leafless. The person was drawn as an impoverished "stick" figure, although the therapist had suggested that stick figures were not to be utilized for this exercise. The person lacked hands and feet as well as facial features.

The anorectic chooses to "restrict" herself in her art expression in a way that parallels the way she lives her life—in the starvation of her body and the strict controls maintained over her affect. She also views the world in a dichotomous fashion: everything is either black or white, one is either fat or thin, kind or mean, successful or a failure. Therefore, it is an important goal for the art therapist to aid in broadening the patient's range of perception. This is approached symbolically by encouraging her to experiment in her art expression with a wide range of colors, media, and space.

Body Image

The eating-disordered patient's life is based on certain faulty assumptions that need to be exposed and corrected. A primary misconception is that thinness is of magical and inestimable value. For the anorectic patient in particular, this is accompanied by a disturbance of body image of delusional proportions. In addition, there exists a disturbed perception, interpretation, and response to internal body sensations.

The patient's distorted body-image perception is illustrated by a "self-portrait" done by Terry, a 22-year-old anorectic (Figure 3.2). Although she entered the hospital because her emaciation was life-threatening, she viewed herself as obese. Terry's drawings are childlike, lacking indications of her sexuality and thereby suggesting her fears of maturation. The inclusion of a belly button additionally suggests dependency issues. The long neck is evidence of her mind/body separation. The literature on anorexia nervosa states that an intellectualized, mechanistic view of the body must be maintained in order to exert the tremendous amount of willpower necessary to carry out the self-starvation regimes of these young women. The mouth in Terry's drawing is extended beyond the boundaries of the face, first as a smile, then turning to a frown. This is evidence of her intensely oral focus, and her ambivalence about a façade that is generally maintained.

Suzanne, the 39-year-old anorectic, made a self-portrait that revealed herself as fat and childlike, with body contours that are amorphous and ill-defined

(Figure 3.3, p. 56). She lacks hands or feet, symbolic of the extreme feelings of ineffectiveness and impotence in the world, yet her face contains a "smile," illustrating a compensatory defense. The patient made repeated references during the course of treatment to her abhorrence of feeling "pregnant." The onset of her anorexia coincided with traumatic events related to a pregnancy 20 years earlier.

A primary therapeutic goal is to assist these patients in correlating their body-image distortions with their feelings of personal ineffectiveness and inadequacy, and to break through the denial of those feelings. In this case, Suzanne was able to acknowledge that underneath her smiling exterior, she views herself as "mean," "ugly," "fat," "stupid," "worthless," "no good," "insecure," and most important, "guilty." It is notable that this new acknowledgement of painful feelings coincided with an expansion in her use of space in the art. This was contrary to earlier drawings which were comprised of empty space and small tentative forms that mirrored her own self-effacement and denial of feelings.

Figure 3.2. Self-portrait

Figure 3.3.   Self-portrait

Ventilation of Feelings

A major therapeutic task is to help the anorectic in a search for autonomy and self-directed identity. Experiences of failure in self-expression, along with the incorporation of defective concepts and tools for organizing and expressing needs, have led to bewilderment and confusion in dealing with others. Therapeutic focus therefore is directed towards evoking awareness of impulses, feelings, and needs that have been denied and their safe and appropriate expression.

New media are purposefully introduced into the sessions to support risk-taking and feelings of achievement as patients master new artistic skills. Suzanne was encouraged to use more colors and space on the page through the introduction of collage media. She was instructed to *pick out magazine pictures of "how she was feeling."* In response to the directive, her entire collection of images were of food, surrounding a central image of an obese woman that she claimed was herself. This early identification of feelings focuses on self-directed rage through a delusional image of herself as fat. When she suddenly realized that anger could be released through the art, she furiously scribbled over the entire collage with a black crayon, attempting to symbolically wipe herself out of existence.

The difficulty the anorectic has in recognizing and expressing internal feeling states is partly related to the initial failure in the preverbal infant stage, which results in a defect in verbalizing these emotions. Sours (1980) conceptualized this central issue as a failure in the developmental stage of separation/individuation, as theorized by Mahler (1972).

Wolfe et al. (1985) posits that "art as an expressive medium has certain distinct advantages. Fundamentally, art has a concrete, kinesthetic, and tangible quality of expressiveness that words lack. . . . A feeling or attitude, symbolized and represented on paper or in clay, can be literally seen, touched, and acknowledged as words cannot. A picture may be worth a thousand words, but . . . more importantly, a picture may express what the patient lacks words to describe" (p. 198).

Art was used to stimulate the externalization and reflection of internal feeling states and attitudes for Sarah, age 23. She was encouraged to *depict feelings you have had recently in the form of a feeling chart* (Figure 3.4). Previously engaged in the denial of any affectual responses, Sarah successfully identified her emotions as "depression, sadness, hate, love, anger, and hurt" and shared them with the group. By giving this directive in a group situation, the therapist can help anorectics begin to see that they are not alone in their uncomfortable feelings.

Figure 3.4. Feeling chart

Family Dynamic Issues

The theory that as a child the preanorectic feels controlled by her parents is supported in the literature. Some of the authors identify a domineering, rejecting mother in an achievement-oriented family (Bruch, 1973). In other cases there is a controlling, perfectionistic father or both parents are overprotective and controlling with their "ideal" child. In these families, the appearance of being the "perfect" family is frequently kept up at all costs. Family dynamics as described by Minuchin, Rosman, and Baker (1978) include the characteristics of enmeshment, rigidity, overprotectiveness, and poor conflict resolution. The anorectic is involved in unresolved conflict through triangulation, detouring, or a stable, enmeshed coalition with one parent.

The emerging anorectic may develop the following characteristics: excessive devotion to work or school; depression; feelings of powerlessness; low self-esteem; inability of self-assertion; perfectionism; obsessive-compulsive behaviors; and a denial of her sexual self. Feeling out of control in what is perceived as a "no-win" situation with her family, the anorectic ultimately directs her energy towards controlling the size and shape of her body mechanistically, through strenuous dieting and fasting behaviors. As a "successful dieter" she begins to feel more powerful and indeed gains power by controlling the whole family's involvement with food. As her ensuing starvation becomes life-threatening, it becomes a focal point within the family of great concern. While starving herself, the individual remains intensely focused on food, often taking over the role of cooking and meal planning for the family and developing compulsive, ritualistic behaviors, such as the hoarding of food. The anorectic gains the attention of family members as they concentrate and comment on her actions; therefore, she develops a vigilance over her actions and an obsessive concern for perfection.

Note that there is a range of ages along which anorexic symptoms may begin to emerge: from early adolescence, which often coincides with pubertal onset, through young adulthood. Developmental tasks of separation and individuation are experienced as overwhelming stressors to the preanorectic as she attempts such things as dating, going to college, or getting a job. The onset of anorexia nervosa after early adulthood appears rare; however, once established, symptoms may persist well into adulthood. Without successful clinical intervention, symptoms will often continue to increase in severity until the patient's life is ended.

When Terry was asked to *draw her family*, she made two images. In the first, there was a depiction of the family constellation before Terry entered the hospital. The patient is portrayed as separated from her parents and in alliance with her boyfriend; the parents' marital separation and her mother's alcohol abuse are also depicted. In the second drawing, Terry depicted the family once her illness had been recognized as life-threatening and she had entered the hospital. The boyfriend had been discarded as parents were brought together again in an effort to save her. The patient had drawn herself in a childlike, dependent position, supported physically on either side by her parents, with feet that did not reach the ground. Terry had discovered a powerful way to control family dynamics and to bring her parents back from the brink of divorce. Tragically, the price she was paying for the attention and for keeping her family "together" was her own self-destruction.

A striking portrayal of a mother-daughter relationship was made by Amy, age 24. She symbolized her mother as a large mouth in the process of "swallowing" the patient. Her sister was near her on the right, throwing her a life preserver. Amy viewed this as symbolizing her sister's helpful façade in her own attempt to also "control" the patient. The patient's father, drawn almost invisibly in the far upper righthand corner, was seen as emotionally absent and uninvolved.

Sarah, age 23, depicted her view of her stepfather as controlling the family, as he symbolically threatened to "put everyone in a box and lock it up" (Figure 3.5). He is a much larger, more intimidating figure than the others. Sarah stated that she felt frightened by him and later revealed his history of physically abusive actions toward her. At the same time she admitted being drawn to his caring side; this was symbolized in the artwork by the heart in his foot.

Figure 3.5.   My family?

Issues of Control

Typically the enmeshed, anorexic family system responds to stresses brought on by developmental changes of family members with greater rigidity rather than flexibility. Instead of fostering continued growth and autonomy, such a family "becomes a cage" (Munuchin, Rosman, & Baker, 1978).

The anorectic learns to maintain control over the family environment and herself through fasting; this control becomes internalized to the point that spontaneity is lost. Anorectics experience their minds and their bodies as separate entities, and they feel driven to control the unruly and despised body (Bruch, 1978). The feeling of being trapped was depicted by Suzanne with a photograph of a caged tiger over which bars were drawn. Other patients typically portrayed themselves with their bodies in chains. These images are indicative of the underlying intense emotions over which the patient feels strict control must be maintained.

Issues with control are quickly transposed onto the hospital environment. Terry's view of her relationship with her doctor was portrayed in a collage image as a power struggle in which the patient was portrayed as shrinking, and her doctor was seen as "bigger than life." Terry entitled this picture "Overpowering and controlling someone who has no control or is powerless," and stated that she wanted to "feel more of an equal person." She was beginning to confront the role she played in her relationships and to realize that she was not merely being "victimized." It was essential for Terry to change her maladaptive behaviors to bring about healthier ways of relating to others.

Cognitive Distortions

Bruch (1978) believes that psychotherapy with anorectics should be a process that facilitates recognizing and challenging erroneous assumptions and attitudes so that they can be abandoned. These assumptions and attitudes usually are a reflection of the following cognitive patterns: dichotomous thinking, overgeneralization, "should" statements, superstitious thinking, and personalization.

Art therapy directives can be utilized to concretize the learning process and to practice new, healthier ways of thinking. Superstitious thinking, overgeneralization, and personalization can all be addressed and challenged. This is done through art tasks that direct the patient to depict situations where there is both cause and effect. For example, in superstitious thinking there is a perceived cause and effect relationship between unrelated events, such as "If I lose weight, I will have a career and people will like me." Overgeneralization results from perceiving small, usually negative, events as setting off a chain of endless repetition. For example, a small setback in eating behavior is generalized to "I'll never get better, my eating will never improve" (Burns, 1980). Personalization is the perception of oneself as the focus of other people's attention, with the result of taking events personally. Therefore, weight gain may be the perceived cause of people's laughing and whispering as the anorectic walks by.

Dichotomous thinking is based on extreme perceptions of the world, without recognizing the existence of a middle range; for example, everything is perceived as all-black, or all-white. This can be confronted with "shades of grey" art tasks. Directives that encourage a broadened range of perception are used. Patients may be asked to illustrate spectrums of emotions, movements, body sizes, colors, shapes, sizes, textures, and so on.

Dichotomous cognitions and body-image distortions were both explored in drawing exercises done by Suzanne (Figure 3.6). She was told to *depict a woman who is too fat, one who is too skinny, and one who is medium weight.* Her sketch of the *too fat* woman was done with ease, and it is noteworthy that this woman's weight was the same as Suzanne's target weight, which she had resisted achieving. The *too skinny* woman was difficult for Suzanne to produce; she said that "it is impossible to be too skinny." However, it is interesting to note that in her depiction, this woman's weight was the same as her own upon admission to the hospital. The woman whose weight was medium or just right was the hardest for

Figure 3.6. The whale

Suzanne to create. However, when she did so, the figure was assigned the weight of 95 pounds, which was Suzanne's present weight. She acknowledged that she was adjusting to the idea that a heavier weight might be acceptable to her. Yet her continued conflict is indicated in her drawing title "The Whale."

Self-image was explored by Sarah, as it related to movement, joy, and pleasure. The directive emerged as a result of a disturbing dream in which the patient had viewed her own body, no longer distorted as to weight or shape, but as a separate entity, unable to provide her joy or pleasure. Sarah wanted to make an ally out of her body, rather than viewing it mechanistically, or as separate from herself. Therefore, she was instructed to *visualize, and then depict herself moving for the sake of pleasure.*

Sarah spent some time with an anatomy book, then drew the movement images in sequence over the course of three sessions (Figure 3.7). Sarah was gratified and admitted that she felt much closer to her body as a result of this exercise, which she entitled "Metamorphosis." The final picture in the series relates back to the first dream image. The ghostlike form in the dream has been given an identity, representing Sarah's healthier integration of body and mind. As she "reclaimed" her body through this exercise, a new sense of ease was reflected both in her portrayal of herself as progressively less encumbered by clothing and also by the appropriate inclusion of sexual characteristics.

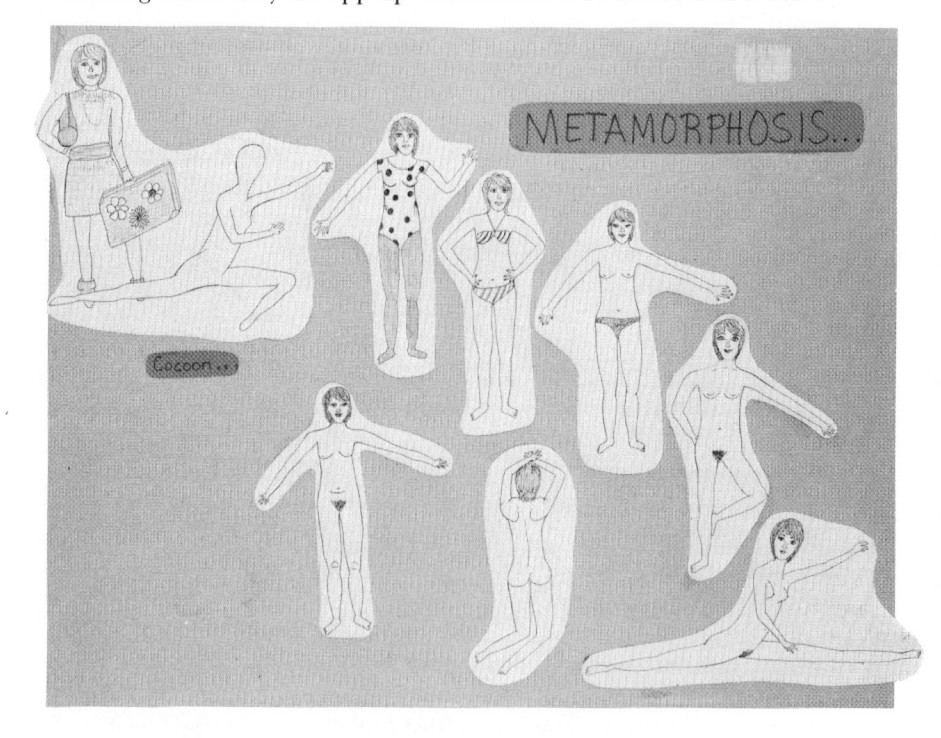

Figure 3.7.   Metamorphosis

Personal Effectiveness

The anorexic patient's self-esteem is enhanced as she learns new skills; practices problem-solving techniques; and becomes more confident in her decision-making skills. Many art directives focus on confronting problems and exploring their solutions.

Terry did problem-solving exercises to reduce anxiety about newly acquired meal planning responsibilities. She "practiced" making her choices for the following day's meals through collage. During this task Terry planned to have oatmeal with milk for breakfast, a hamburger for lunch, and soup and salad for dinner. This type of rehearsal lowers the anorectic's anxieties because she exchanges complusive, ritualistic behaviors, such as counting calories or hoarding food, for appropriate healthy behaviors, such as learning how to determine appropriate portion sizes and nutritional choices.

Individuation

Eating-disordered patients experience difficulties with separation and individuation. Often this results from earlier, overly enmeshed family dynamics, dependency issues, and difficulty in the expression of feelings. Therefore, intensified socialization and bonding experiences are made available through the art therapy modality. Art tasks are especially designed to enable patients (1) to review their hospitalization, (2) to promote further integration of important learning experiences, and (3) for closure. In a positive separation experience these individuals are able to acknowledge the work they have done and to express feelings towards other patients and staff members. This will help to reinforce the adaptive learning experiences they have had and to encourage a healthier step toward autonomy.

It is essential in a hospital setting to include saying good-bye to the other patients and hospital staff, both pictorially and verbally. Farewell group meetings may be held, in which patients create and exchange pictures that portray their feelings for one another. They keep the pictures as visual, tangible reminders of their relationships. Specific directives for farewell group sessions will be given in a later section of this chapter. Since the anorectics have been encouraged to regain control in positive, adaptive ways, their plans for employment or school, along with living arrangements, are also worked upon simultaneously in individual sessions during the termination phase of treatment.

In preparing for her life outside of the hospital as an independent, autonomous adult, Suzanne was told to *depict a problem she expects to encounter, and how she plans to resolve it.* Her art revealed the upcoming "problem" of "finding a job" and her hopes of working in theater or the film industry. This was represented by a picture of actors on a movie set. Next to this image Suzanne drew her solutions: to send out her resume, to go on interviews, and to pray. When the patient focused on the solution part of the exercise, she began to recognize her fears about leaving the hospital, which until now had remained unconscious. These fears were manifested in the art both by her regressive drawing style and also by the intimidating costumed figures, which she had chosen to represent movie actors.

When Amy was preparing to leave the hospital, issues of separation and individuation were assessed. She was instructed to *depict how you see yourself one year from now* (Figure 3.8). In the next year, Amy portrayed herself as working full time; vacationing; accepting her now normal body weight; enjoying buying new clothes; and, perhaps most dramatically, beginning to date again. It had been years since she had participated in such activities due to her illness. This type of art directive supports the patient's potential for continued growth outside of the hospital setting by bringing both reality and motivation to the forefront.

Figure 3.8.   How I see myself one year from now

BULIMIA NERVOSA: DIAGNOSTIC CRITERIA

The *Diagnostic and Statistical Manual of Mental Disorders,* or *DSM-III-R* (American Psychiatric Association, 1987), cites the following diagnostic criteria for bulimia' nervosa:

A. Recurrent episodes of binge eating (rapid consumption of a large amount of food in a discrete period of time).
B. A feeling of lack of control over eating behavior during the eating binges.
C. The person regularly engages in either self-inducted vomiting, use of laxatives or diuretics, strict dieting or fasting, or vigorous exercise in order to prevent weight gain.
D. A minimum average of two binge eating episodes a week for a least three months.
E. Persistent overconcern with body shape and weight. (pp. 68–69)*

*Reprinted with permission from The American Psychiatric Association.

Although the anorexic patient maintains extreme and rigid control over her body and eating behaviors, the bulimic patient, in contrast, often views herself as an "unsuccessful anorectic." There is a constant struggle with her impulses in an attempt to gain control over her eating behavior. Overwhelmed by, and giving in to, impulses to binge, she purges either with vomiting or laxatives to control her weight. For many patients a shift eventually occurs in which patients begin to binge in order to purge, rather than vice versa, because of the relief and euphoria they experience from the purging behavior.

The binge-purge cycle becomes all-consuming due to the excessive amount of time that is spent in shopping, preparing, and eating the food, and then purging, with the cycle repeating itself anywhere from one to 20 times daily. The patient also goes to great lengths to maintain secrecy, due to the tremendous feelings of shame and humiliation about her behavior. She may have great financial difficulties brought on by having to buy the vast amounts of food that she consumes, and she may resort to stealing and shoplifting. Other self-destructive "binge-type" behaviors may also be present, such as bouts with drugs or alcohol, or sexual acting out.

ART PSYCHOTHERAPY WITH THE BULIMIC

Assessment

Sandy, a 20-year-old bulimic patient, produced a House-Tree-Person drawing during the initial assessment phase of therapy (Figure 3.9). The utilization

Figure 3.9.   House-tree-person assesssment drawing

of space on the page, as well as the presence of color, produces a sharp contrast to the typical assessment drawings done by the anorexic patient. Sandy began drawing the *house* first, by using a ruler, marking the straight edges with controlled precision. Unable to maintain these self-imposed controls, she soon discarded the ruler and began to draw in a more anxious, and progressively less controlled fashion, spilling out her imagery until the entire page was filled in. Psychological indicators in the drawing of the house include a powerful fantasy life (suggested by emphasized detail work on the roof) and fused boundaries with another family member (implied by duality in the house structure). Acting-out tendencies are suggested in the tree drawing, which leans to the left (Buck, 1974). Her person representation was claimed as a "self-image" and elicited great anxiety as she erased and redrew the image many times over. The end result showed her "body" completely hidden behind the tree, which Sandy said represented her desire "to hide and not be seen."

Allison, age 18, a bulimic patient with a history of prior anorexic symptoms, drew a House-Tree-Person picture in a childlike style (Figure 3.10). The patient

Figure 3.10.   House-tree-person assessment drawing

associated to the depiction as being a scene from her past, saying, "when I was six, we were happy then . . . this was right before we moved away and my bulimic symptoms began." Maturity fears are suggested by the fixation on an earlier time in her life. Family secrets are evident, as witnessed by the attic window, closed window shades, and "X" in the garage roof. A symbiotic relationship is strongly indicated by the following dualities: a double structured house and garage and double branches in the tree.

Related to the keeping of family secrets is the use of denial as defense; this is evidenced by the appearance of a "picture perfect house" and the "decorative" surface details such as flowers, shrubs, and window curtains.

Self-Image and Body Image

The self-portrait done by Laura, age 23, illustrates her relationship to the binge-purge cycle, a secret that she perceives as humiliating and all engrossing (Figure 3.11). The toilet bowl looms large, covering most of the space on the page. Laura portrays herself as tiny and childlike, which is indicative of maturity fears and a prepubertal self-image. The figure, which is drawn from behind and facing into the toilet bowl, reveals her inability to face the world, along with her obsessional, addictive relationship to her purging behavior.

Figure 3.11.   Self-portrait

Laura was then asked *to draw how she could help herself with this binge-purge problem.* She responded that she could help herself by "expressing my feelings, not keeping them bottled up inside me." Her artwork shows herself talking things over with her roommate at the hospital. The patient also included the following solutions: 1) "get rid of need to punish bad self"; 2) "like myself"; 3) "expel rotted core"; and 4) "do artwork." Laura's poor self-image was graphically underscored by her rendition of floating heads suggestive of body-mind separation. Also, her unconscious omission of eyes implies a generalized ineffectiveness, and undiscriminating tendencies, as mentioned by Ogden (1981).

Two weeks later, Laura made a picture that revealed both her extreme ambivalence about growing up and her struggle with out-of-control behaviors. In this collage, she portrayed herself initially as a young woman who she described as being "too sophisticated, sexy, and wild." The patient explained that this is the image that she presents to the world through her looks, style of dress, and acting-out behaviors, such as drug abuse and sexual encounters. In the photograph her hands were in her pockets, revealing feelings of powerlessness and evasiveness, and delinquent behaviors (Machover, 1949).

In the collage, the magazine cutout of a small child running away with her back turned was her "true self," afraid of growing up and taking on the responsibilities and autonomy of young womanhood. In addition, "out-of-control" feelings were symbolized by a car careening toward the figures, as well as by her caption, "Make a mistake tonight."

Images of children remain a constant theme for many of the bulimics. Helping these patients to grieve for the loss of their childhood and to face their fears of maturation is an important therapeutic task for this population.

Family Dynamic Issues

Similar to the family dynamic profile of the anorexic patient, issues of control and expectations of achievement are also paramount features of the bulimic's family profile. Enmeshment of boundaries between parent and child are often present, although coping patterns may be somewhat different. The anorexic family system places a high value on conflict avoidance and the appearance of a "perfect" family, thus exhibiting the phenomenon of pseudo-mutuality. In contrast, many bulimic family systems expose their conflicts, since the children tend to be openly rebellious. Histories of family obesity, depression, and alcoholism are common. The emerging bulimic, like the anorectic, experiences feelings of depression, powerlessness, and low self-esteem. Nevertheless, she is more likely to respond with acting-out behavior than with passivity or withdrawal.

The following drawings done by Allison show the bulimic's family enmeshment issues as they are typified in the art. Because of the suggestion of a dysfunctional, enmeshed relationship gathered from Allison's House-Tree-

Person assessment drawing (refer to Figure 3.10), she was asked in a follow-up session to *depict a relationship she has with a significant-other person* (Figure 3.12). In this picture Allison has metaphorically portrayed her relationship to her mother. This parent is symbolized by the barbwire fence, and Allison herself is symbolized by the tree. She believed that the fence was restricting the growth and development of the tree. When asked about the blood she had drawn on the fence, she replied, "That represents the pain that I cause my mother, I mean my mother causes me." Although therapeutic progress had been made regarding increased self-esteem, the symbiotic tie, as evidenced in the drawing and by her Freudian slip, was still unresolved, and issues of separation and individuation remained critical for this patient.

Allison was asked to *solve the problem of how the tree could gain autonomy and separate from the fence.* She began by cutting open the gate and folding it back, symbolically making a way to free the tree. At this point she said that it appeared that the foundation, or trunk, of the tree was intertwined with the fence. By separating the tree and the fence, the foundation would be lost and the tree would be unable to stand.

Without any suggestions from the therapist, Allison quickly began to redraw a new trunk, declaring that it would "be up to the tree to form a new foundation," that is, to create a new identity that was not fused to her mother. Filling in the void left by the separation of the fence and the tree with a new trunk, Allison let out a cathartic sigh in response to her metaphoric practice of the separation process.

Figure 3.12.   My relationship with my mother

Ventilation of Feelings and Issues of Control

Sandy, age 23, was asked to *make a chart showing six feelings you've had recently* (Figure 3.13). She started the drawing in the upper lefthand corner in a controlled fashion, using a ruler to delineate her feelings of depression. On the center, lefthand side of the page, a spiral drawn inward indicates her depression, with possible suicidal intent. The clown in the middle of the drawing is found by this author to be a common bulimic symbol, expressive of the happy exterior and the masking of underlying feelings. As anger began to surface, Sandy lost control of the sketch and frenetically scribbled over the page. She "wiped out" her previous images and then began to cut the paper with scissors. Finally, she took out a previously hidden cigarette lighter and prepared to burn a hole in the paper!

The patient was admonished to "stop what she was doing immediately." She was asked to relinquish the lighter, as it was forbidden on the unit. Since she needed to learn how to regain control, Sandy was told to *create a picture that will help her to regain self-composure and control over her impulses.* Again using the ruler, the patient formed a geometric design, utilizing all of the space on the page. She created symbolic boundaries, then carefully filled in the outlined shapes with color. Sandy was relieved when she discovered how the art served as a holding device. She affirmed that this technique would be used in the future to keep destructive impulses in check.

Figure 3.13.   Feeling chart

The following week, Sandy came to the session directly after lunch. She declared that she had a strong desire to act out by "purging" her lunch, but had so far resisted and had chosen to come to the art therapy session instead. She then asked for the box of magazine pictures and, at the suggestion of the therapist, involved herself in creating a symbolic "binge-purge" collage (Figure 3.14). Once again she experienced a catharsis due to the emotional purging afforded by the art process, along with the healing aspect of sharing her pain with the therapist. Sandy revealed that she also felt a heightened sense of per-

Figure 3.14.   Binge-purge collage

sonal effectiveness because of the healthy and creative way she had found to resolve her immediate self-destructive impulses.

Cognitive Distortions

Faulty cognitions are a problem for bulimic patients. However, their thought and body-image distortions are usually less extreme than those of the anorectics and must be evaluated on an individual basis. To confront both polarized cognitions and body-image distortions, Laura was told *to represent: women who are too thin; women who are just right;* and *women who are too fat.* Laura made three collages, one for each category of women. Thinness was clearly viewed in a very desirable light by this patient; next to photos of extremely slender women was a row of male judges and the caption, "These *thin* women are being toasted by the men."

In the second picture, Laura's difficulty with accepting the possibility of a middle-range vis-à-vis body image was evident. Although she chose photographs to represent women with "just right" bodies, she then encircled those body areas that she perceived as flawed or too fat.

The third collage was the easiest for Laura to produce. She explained that the women in the photographs were too heavy in the hips, thighs, and breasts. Because of this, she fantasized that they were forced to "take their brothers to the prom."

Individuation

Work on resolving family dynamics remained a salient goal in Allison's treatment plan. As she tried to confront her need to gain autonomy, she experienced repeated setbacks. These were manifested through bouts of depression and urges to fall back into bingeing and purging behaviors. To readdress separation issues, the patient was told to *make a drawing of her family.* In the art her mother and father were displayed as roses, thorny and closed. The patient is. seen as a butterfly flying into an ominous black cloud, and her younger brother is portrayed as a snail sitting next to mother and father. A thunderbolt coming out of the cloud is aimed directly at her younger brother, the snail (Figure 3.15a). This is representative of Allison's rage toward her sibling, who was replacing her in getting the family's attention. The patient stated that the large yellow raindrops represented her "tears of sadness" and the black cloud was her "depression."

Because of a concern about the large size of the black cloud, which was a metaphor for Allison's depression, the therapist directed her to *represent, in storyboard fashion, what happens to the butterfly as it nears the black cloud.* In Allison's initial response, the butterfly entered the black cloud, yet although immersed in it, it remained intact. The next serial drawing showed the wings of the butterfly completely blackened. This represented the overwhelming depression and the patient's inability to defend against it. Yet the butterfly's central golden core remained uncontaminated, thus offering some vestiges of hope (Figure 3.15b).

Allison's final drawing of the series required several attempts and a great deal of effort (Figure 3.15c). In this image Allison illustrated the cental core of the butterfly as breaking free from its depression-soaked wings. It is heading into a symbolically desirable, flowered landscape, where it can begin the work of reconstructing its "depression-free" wings.

Once again, through the use of the metaphor, Allison was able to reach into her unconscious and examine the seriousness of her dejection as it related to separation and individuation issues. The picture of winning the battle over her depression had a profound effect upon Allison. It gave her renewed confidence in her ability to get through the crisis phase in treatment.

GROUP ART THERAPY TECHNIQUES

The art therapy techniques presented in this chapter can be adapted for work with eating-disordered patients on a group basis as well as on an individual basis. Group work with anorectics and bulimics offers a number of benefits in several areas, which are delineated herein.

Social bonding skills are promoted as group members experience working on jointly created tasks, sharing space graphically, making group decisions on projects, exchanging feedback with other participants, and having a positive, social experience.

Commitment to the therapy process is promoted, particularly for new patients, who are typically resistant to giving up their illness. When they interact with members who have progressed and attained a working alliance to the group, they can then foresee the possibility of their own gains. As hope is instilled, they are supported to make the same commitment for themselves. Additionally, the more experienced patients benefit from an increase in self-esteem as they become aware of their own growth in relationship to the newer patients. They are frequently placed into leadership roles and gain greater confidence in their abilities.

Educationally, group treatment allows anorectics and bulimics to learn from one another at different stages of recovery and to model healthier skills. Because of the simultaneous expression of feelings afforded by group art tasks, patients discover that they are not alone in their feelings and are able to provide mutual support in breaking through their patterns of loneliness and isolation. As stated by Yalom (1975), it is not uncommon for a patient to benefit by observing the therapy of another patient with a similar problem constellation; this is referred to as "vicarious" or "spectator" therapy. "Even if specific imitative behavior is short-lived, it may function to help the individual unfreeze by experimenting with new behavior" (p. 17).

Figure 3.15(a).   Family drawing

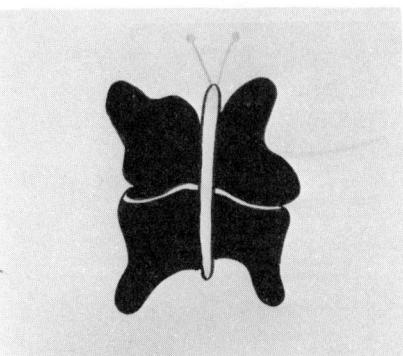

Figure 3.15(b).   The wings of the butterfly

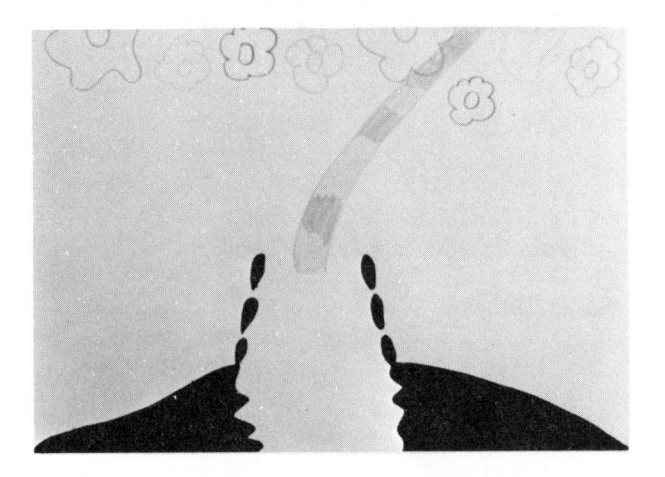

Figure 3.15(c).   Breaking free

Because the patients first express themselves in their art, and then verbally, and because many art tasks are designed for collaborative work, modeling and imitation features occur on many levels. Perceptual distortions are confronted with efficacy. Faulty cognitive patterns such as overgeneralization, dichotomous thinking, and personalization can be pointed out by peers; also, healthier thought constructs can be observed and adapted. Body-image distortions can also be challenged by group members. Although extreme in many cases, particularly for the anorectics, these perceptual distortions do not typically occur in relationship to others' body shapes. For example, a patient who erroneously sees herself as fat will not also view others with similar body dimensions as overweight. A measure of reality testing is introduced by the group process, as participants who see themselves as too fat are confronted by each other on these distorted perceptions.

The following examples are of group art therapy tasks designed for social bonding, sharing, expressing emotions, problem solving, confrontation of body image, and mastery of media. The directives mentioned may be utilized in both inpatient and outpatient settings and for groups with anorectic or bulimic patients. An optimal group size is four to six patients.

Group Tasks

Group members are instructed to *create a mural together, using markers or crayons,* or to *choose a three-dimensional medium and create an art product together.* Media such as marking pens, crayons, pastels, magazine pictures and other collage media, construction paper, and plasticene may also be made available. The group is instructed to *work together and to problem solve either verbally or silently.*

An example of this technique is illustrated by a group of four anorectic patients. They chose tissue paper collage as their medium and worked nonverbally to create a mural. They placed a large sheet of paper between them on the floor. Initially all of the patients worked fastidiously and in an isolated manner. Each person took over a corner of the paper and carefully cut out squares of tissue paper, making certain not to intrude upon each other's territory as they did the pasting. As the page became nearly filled, the members were forced to gather closer together. It was at this point that they broke through their reserve and began to reach over and around each other to apply their pieces of collage. In an amiable manner, they began to help each other, and with new inspiration they spontaneously began to tear, rather than cut out, the paper pieces. The group finished the project amid gales of laughter and proudly titled the piece "Getting Together." The members reported that they had enjoyed the collaborative process. They realized that the physical contact had also helped them to break through their barriers of isolation.

Another hospital group of four members was told to *work together to create an art object from a cardboard box* and to discuss a problem-solving procedure (Figure 3.16). The patients decided that each person should be responsible for decorating one side of the box. They would then work together to decorate the top. As the group proceeded, the three anorexic patients were extremely careful about staying within the limits of the space they were allocated. Nevertheless, the bulimic patient had some difficulty in maintaining her boundaries. As she spray-painted her side of the box, she began to splatter paint over the entire box, much to her peers' dismay. They were able to confront her appropriately and to offer problem-solving suggestions. The group continued to practice their communication skills as they worked together to finish decorating the top of the box.

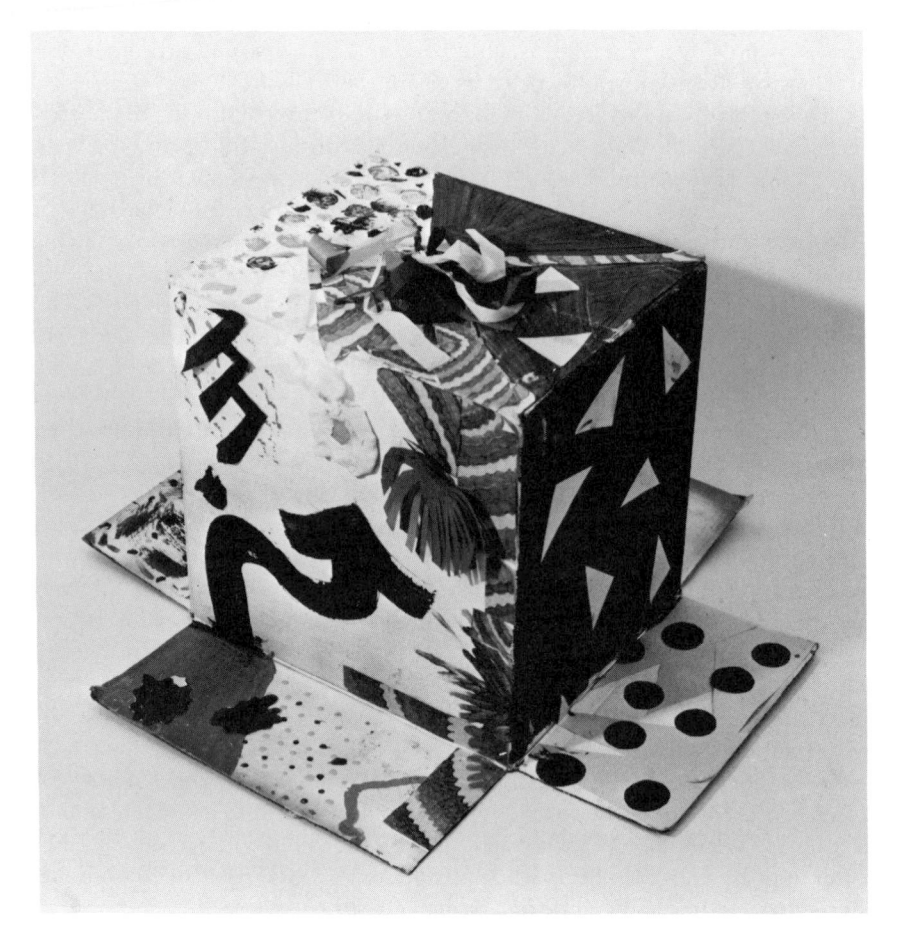

Figure 3.16.   Group task: art object

Body Tracings

Body tracing is an exercise which is intended to break through the maladaptive coping mechanisms of the eating-disordered patient on many levels. Most important body-image distortions are addressed, as this powerful exercise allows for externalization, and the patients are able to view their bodies objectively. Boundary issues are viewed along with issues of control. The patient is prompted to look at feelings and impulses as they arise from within, then to confront her mechanistic manipulation of body shape in an attempt to solve psychological dilemmas. The body-tracing exercise is especially valuable when done in the group context, since the usual resistance to the exercise can be overcome with group support. Social interaction and bonding are encouraged as patients work with partners during the tracing phase. In the sharing period, the multiple drawings provide a dramatic visual impact, and reality testing is promoted as tracings are discussed and feedback is given.

Two or three sessions are required for the completion of this single exercise. Patients are asked to come to the first session wearing formfitting clothing, such as leotards. Looser garments are brought along, to be worn after the tracing is completed. Large sheets of butcher-block paper are taped on the walls or doorways, and the group is divided into teams of two. Partners take turns tracing around each others' bodies as carefully and accurately as possible.

The next part of the project requires that the body tracings be filled in. The patients are directed to *portray their feelings symbolically within the frame of their body tracing*. This technique gives the participants a way to gain awareness of the emotions that reside within their bodies and then to ventilate these hidden feelings. All types of media are made available and several sessions may be required for this project.

The finished artwork is displayed on the wall. Members are asked to *share their self-portraits along with the feelings that have been evoked by this task*. Sandy's self-portrait is one example of this directive. As she worked on her tracing with marking pens, paints, and tissue paper collage, she claimed, "I just had fun and tried not to think about it too much" (Figure 3.17). However, her self-awareness increased as she shared her portrait with the group. Sandy realized that the translucent tissue paper section, from the left shoulder through the digestive tract and stomach region, represented "the opening-up" process that she was going through in therapy. She continued on, stating that the more risks she took to reveal her feelings, the fewer bulimic urges were experienced. The patient also correlated a decrease in body-image distortion with her new attempts at expressing her emotions. Sandy recounted that as she "sat on her feelings," her body appeared larger to her, particularly her thighs. However, after identifying her emotions, her body "appeared to actually shrink in size!!!"

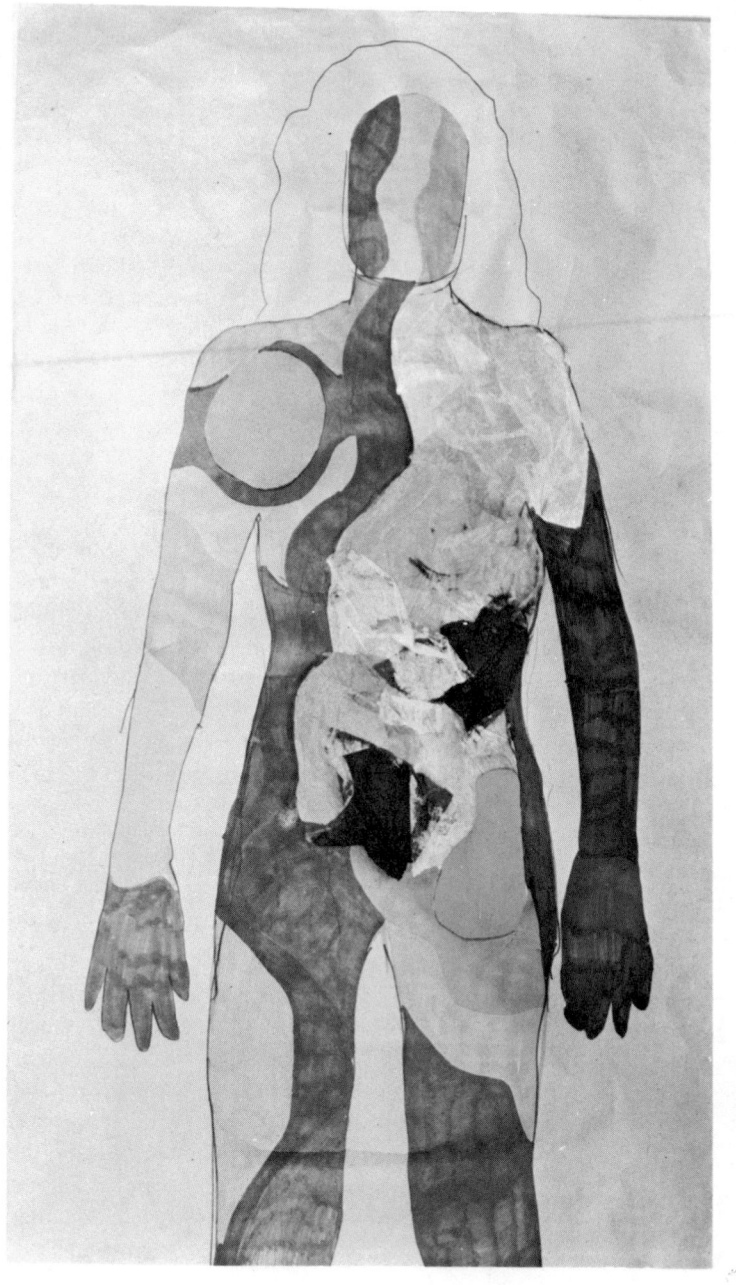

Figure 3.17.   Body tracing

Sandy wondered why she had delineated three sections in portraying her face. It was noted that the color of these sections were green, yellow, and red, similar to those of a traffic signal. Sandy then related the symbolism to issues of self-control and the continual state of conflict over whether or not to give in to the bulimic urges. When the patient noted that her hands were colored in green, she commented on the addictive quality of her illness by stating, "My hands respond to my impulses with a green light, while my head is still thinking whether to stop or go."

Sandy gained new insights and greater acceptance of her body size as normal after viewing her body objectively through this exercise. Feedback from peers concurred with her insight that weight loss was a misdirected and inappropriate concern. She voiced a wish to shift her focus to other areas of her life such as taking risks with emotional expression, improving communication skills, working out family problems, and making choices regarding her education and career.

Separation

Acknowledging the bonding that has occurred between the patients is a very important part of the separation process. This is true whether it is a hospital or an outpatient experience. With termination there are two directives that help to provide concrete acknowledgment of the relationships that have formed.

The first is a "Good-Bye Gift Box" that is made for the departing group member. The art therapist begins by rendering a large gift box on a sheet of paper. Then each member is asked to *place a symbol within the box of something you would like to give or communicate to the departing member.* It can be *a symbol of your feelings for the person who is leaving.* The person who is leaving is asked to *make a picture communicating how you feel about each of the participants, and your experiences with them while in the group.*

When Laura was leaving after four months of hospitalization, a "Good-Bye Gift Box" was presented to her by the group. It contained a four-leaf clover for good luck, symbols representing the strides she had made in art therapy, and positive wishes for a future that included healthy eating and exercise, moving out of her parents home and into her own apartment, and reenrolling in college. Laura was encouraged to take the gift box home as a group transitional object and the rest of the group was allowed to keep the pictures she made for them. Laura expressed her gratitude for the emotional support she had received during her hospitalization, which was graphically underscored through this exercise.

When a member is leaving, the following task encourages the relating of the shared emotional history of the group. The instructions are (1) to *draw and cut out the shape of their hand* and (2) *to decorate the cutout with a symbol representing themselves.* Afterwards they are to *put their paper hands on a large sheet of paper* that has been placed in the center of the table. This art task is followed by a discussion of the symbols chosen and of the placement of the hands.

Lynn participated in this exercise as she prepared to leave the milieu. She drew a picture of a sun on her hand that represented "feelings of hope" as she looked forward to her life outside the hospital. She placed her "hand" drawing in the center of the paper, making it available for contact from everyone. When Lynn expressed her sadness at saying good-bye, her sentiments were echoed by the group. As the cluster of hands was reviewed, it was noted by the group members that all of the cutouts were touching one another. The patients expressed their joy about the symbolism and about the close relationships they had formed in the group. They exchanged mutual support and encouragement for their continued progress and recovery from their eating disorders.

CONCLUDING REMARKS

The complexity of the clinical factors involved in the treatment of anorexia nervosa and bulimia nervosa have generated a difficult challenge for the mental health professional. The picture of the young woman, normally entering the prime of her life, instead wasting away slowly, inexorably, while family and friends watch helplessly, and the bulimic, destroying her body with endless, compulsive repetitions of bingeing, purging, and laxative abuse—each presents an image of a particularly gripping human tragedy. Today with approximately one million new cases reported by the American Anorexia and Bulimia Association each year, these syndromes represent a significant and urgent health problem.

Although research on the efficacy of various treatment models is growing, what is of particular concern to this author is what appears to be a high recidivism rate, once the patients leave the more structured therapeutic environment. In many cases a pernicious cycle of hospitalization, relapse, and rehospitalization results tragically in the death of the patient. It is critically important that appropriate outpatient care be provided and maintained on a long-term basis for hospitalized patients after discharge.

It is this author's opinion that art psychotherapy offers striking advantages as a treatment modality, whether incorporated into a milieu approach or into an aftercare program. Its strengths as outlined in this chapter include helping the patient to break through patterns of denial and to form a strong therapeutic alliance. It is also instrumental in aiding the patients in establishing a sense of trust in their own feelings, intuitions, and abilities. Issues of self and body image, maladaptive family dynamics, issues of control, of personal effectiveness, and of separation and individuation are more effectively resolved through the incorporation of this modality. It is this author's hope that more and more treatment settings will recognize the strengths of the art psychotherapy modality, and incorporate it as the treatment of choice for these patients.

REFERENCES

American Psychiatric Association. (1987). *Diagnostic and Statistical Manual of Mental Disorders* (Third Edition, Revised). Washington, DC: American Psychiatric Association.

Bruch, H. (1973). *Eating Disorders.* New York: Basic Books.

Bruch, H. (1978). *The Golden Cage. The Enigma of Anorexia Nervosa.* Boston, MA: Harvard University Press.

Brumberg, J. J. (1988). *Fasting Girls.* Cambridge, MA: Harvard University Press.

Buck, J. N. (1974). *The House-Tree-Person Manual Supplement* (4th printing). Beverly Hills, CA: Western Psychological Services.

Burns, R. C., & Kaufman, S. H. (1972). *Actions, Styles and Symbols in Kinetic Family Drawings.* New York: Brunner/Mazel.

Burns, D. (November, 1980). The perfectionist's script for self defeat. *Psychology Today,* pp. 34–52.

Crisp, A. H. (1980). *Anorexia Nervosa: Let Me Be.* New York: Grune & Stratton.

Crowl, N. (1980). Art therapy in patients suffering from anorexia nervosa. *Journal of the Arts in Psychotherapy, 7,* 141–151.

Garfinkel, P. E., & Garner, D. M. (1982). *Anorexia Nervosa: A Multidimensional Perspective.* New York: Brunner/Mazel.

Haeseler, N. (1982). Why are patients with anorexia nervosa responsive to art therapy? In A. DiMara, E. Karmer, & L. Regner (Eds.), *Art Therapy: A Bridge Between Two Worlds.* Falls Church, VA: American Art Therapy Association.

Herzog, D. B., & Copeland, P. M. (1986). Understanding eating disorders. *Family Therapy Today, 1*(4), 3–4.

Kohut, H. (1971). *The Analysis of the Self, 19*(1). New York: International Universities Press.

Machover, K. (1949). *Personality Projection in the Drawing of the Human Figure.* Springfield, IL: Charles C Thomas.

Mahler, M. (1972). On the first three subphases of the separation-individuation process. *International Journal of Psychoanalysis, 53,* 333–338.

Minuchin, S., Rosman, B. L., & Baker, L. (1978). *Psychosomatic Families: Anorexia Nervosa in Context.* Cambridge, MA: Harvard University Press.

Mitchell, D. (1980). Anorexia nervosa. *Arts in Psychotherapy, 7,* 53–60.

Ogden, D. (1981). *Psychodiagnostics and Personality Assessment: A Handbook* (2nd ed.). Los Angeles: Western Psychological Services.

Sargent, J. (1986). Family therapy interventions for anorectics and bulimics. *Family Therapy Today, 1*(4), 1–8.

Sours, J. A. (1980). *Starving to Death in a Sea of Objects: The Anorexia Nervosa Syndrome.* New York: Jason Aronson.

Striegel-Moore, R. H., Silverstein, L. R., French, P., & Rodin, J. (1989). A prospective study of disordered eating among college students. *International Journal of Eating Disorders, 8*(5), 499–509.

Ticen, S. (1990). Feed me . . . cleanse me . . . sexual trauma projected in the art of bulimics. *Journal of the American Art Therapy Association, 7*(1), 17–21.

Wolf, J. M., Willmuth, M. E., Gazda, T., & Watkins, A. (1985). The role of art in the therapy of anorexia nervosa. *International Journal of Eating Disorders, 4*(2), 185–200.

Yalom, I. D. (1975). *The Theory and Practice of Group Psychotherapy* (2nd ed.). New York: Basic Books.

Chapter 4

Art Psychotherapy: An Approach to Borderline Adults

Diane Silverman

During the past two decades psychotherapists, including psychoanalysts, have focused considerable attention on the understanding and treatment of patients demonstrating borderline personality organization. Professionals in all the mental health disciplines encounter borderline patients, often with considerable puzzlement as to how to treat them. The borderline personality organization presents a complex set of dynamics and symptoms that are neither psychotic nor neurotic. There have been numerous attempts by scholarly, experienced clinicians to formulate a cohesive theory of borderline personality organization and a treatment approach to borderline disorders.

Mental health clinicians are faced with the ongoing challenge of understanding this type of personality as well as adapting their knowledge and skills to help these patients understand themselves and function in a more satisfactory and fulfilling way. Since art psychotherapy makes available concrete manifestations of the patient's mental processes, it lends itself to the successful treatment of these individuals. In addition, because of its unique capacity to render or evoke symbols and images related to infantile experience, art therapy is of special value in the treatment of severe pathology connected with primitive mental states. The art therapy modality is particularly effective in supporting the reparative process of those who have experienced early developmental impairment in their object relations.

Bion (1962) proposes that some patients never achieve the capacity to think verbally; they think in images. If they can develop "concrete things" (lines, points, marks on paper, in plastic forms, and so on), they can use those "things" to "think" thoughts in a different way. Eventually, with the help of the therapist, such patients can encode their thoughts and order them in terms of their meaning and importance. Graphic representation of this disordered internal state helps patients to sort out the chaos rather than to experience their mental contents as only sensation-dominated impulses. In this way, the development of cohesion is fostered through a decrease in fragmentation. Due to the concrete mode of structuring the mental state, the patient is able to experience some understanding and containment.

By tapping into the arena of the primal image-sensations of infancy through art, it is possible to retrieve information vital to the treatment of severe psychopathology that originated early in life. The internal states, in particular, of many borderline patients are often difficult, if not impossible, to explain verbally because they are sensation experiences that originate from a time of life prior to the development of language. Their art productions provide an illustration not only of early affective states, but also of defense patterns of fusion and splitting in early object representations.

THE BORDERLINE SYNDROME

Aspects of the borderline syndrome are depicted through the artwork of a patient named Mary. Her art depictions reveal the cold, desolate loneliness and disintegrative anxiety of her internal world, always feeling as if "on the verge of blowing away like a pile of dry autumn leaves into a vacant space" (Figure 4.1). The patient has nothing to hold on to, nothing to contain her fragile and sometimes diffuse sense of self. On the back of her picture, she poignantly conveys her borderline condition in the following poem:

I am a tree
I get confused.
I am a maple tree in autumn
That cannot keep its leaves on . . .
They get loose and then fall off,
Never to return to the place on the tree top.
They scatter around in the crispy breezes
Nothing to anchor themselves to the tree with.
Onto the lawn, onto the roof,
Down the street and stuck to a hoof.
Nothing will hold these pieces together.
For me the fear is that I can't either.

It is difficult for the clinician to describe the borderline character because of the deceptive clinical appearance of inconsistent symptoms in presenting complaints and the wide variability in adaptive areas. The borderline adult patient often describes experiences of emptiness, deadness, aloneness, hopelessness, and dispair. This description is often accompanied later by revelations

Figure 4.1.   I am a tree

of feelings of profound shame and humiliation. Frequently, these patients have difficulty in regulating both their affect and their behavior, and thus exhibit impulsivity in the form of substance abuse, sexual promiscuity or deviation, and multiple, manipulative suicide attempts.

Borderline individuals' weakened ego boundaries give them little capacity for empathic bonding with others. Their relationships are tenuous and shallow and they describe periods of isolation, emotional paralysis and endangerment. These persons have little or no capacity for self-soothing, often turning to drugs or alcohol for this purpose. The disturbance in their relationships frequently takes the form of devaluation, dependency, manipulativeness, and victimization. A longing for closer relationships is in conflict with deep fears of abandonment. Panic states often result whenever the borderline adult experiences an actual or threatened loss of a significant person.

A disruptive emptiness occurs when a borderline patient is deprived of the containing or holding aspects of the treatment (Adler & Buie, 1979). This results in acting-out behavior between sessions, and on the weekends, especially during the therapist's vacations. Any perceived loss is threatening and is manifested in hostility toward the therapist. It is generally exhibited at the end of a session through sarcasm, belligerence, suicidal threats, or the discrediting of interpretations.

Grotstein's (1979, 1982, 1983, 1984a,b) concept of primitive mental states is a useful tool for the understanding of borderline pathology. He describes the borderline personality as comprising a primitive personality that often appears psychotic, and a neurotic or normal one as well. These two personality components have undergone an interpenetration with each other so that a new amalgam emerges that can be described as "primitively neurotic" or "neurotically primitive." It is as if a symbiosis exists between these two "twin" personalities. What particularly distinguishes the borderline personality organization is the capacity of the normal aspects of the personality to contain and repress the "primitive (or psychotic) twin." Art therapy, within this framework, gives access to that part of the individual, the unconscious and sometimes psychotic part of the personality. The artwork of many borderline patients often appears to be typical of the psychotic in both content and structure, despite the relatively normal appearance of the patient. This dual personality development with the primitive component is clearly delineated in a self-portrait produced by Karen, which contrasts a magazine photo of a happy, "normal" woman with a drawing of a terrifying psychotic episode (Figure 4.2).

Figure 4.2.   The dual personality

The borderline suffers from the anxiety of dissolution as a result of the absence of early maternal containment. A threatened separation ultimately refers to a rupture in the primary state of "at-one-ment," or to the defective background object, which evoked a premature psychological birth or sense of "two-ness" (Grotstein 1983, 1984a,b; Tustin 1981). A delay in individuation occurs because of the splitting of the personality and insufficient nurturing. The terror associated with this fear of dissolution is a form of psychological death: a total and absolute aloneness, helplessness and emptiness which has been described as "falling into a bottomless pit."

The borderline has both an "observing ego" and an "experiencing ego." It is the borderline patient's functioning observing ego that differentiates him or her from the psychotic. It is this neurotic part, aware of episodes of fragmentation and decompensation, that can be brought into alliance with the therapist in the treatment process. The observing ego is able to understand interpretations and the purpose of cooperating with the therapist, despite the presence of merger fantasies and primitive mental mechanisms.

The appearance of black holes is very common in the artwork of borderline patients. It is often a characteristic expression of the experience of emptiness, the void, the most profound sense of ultimate danger: a dissolution of the self into a state of mindlessness, meaninglessness, and nothingness (Adler, 1985; Eigen, 1986; Grotstein, 1984b). It represents the ultimate state of disorganization, chaos, randomness, or as Bion (1962, 1963) describes it, as being plunged into the "nameless dread."

The borderline fears a total loss of control that would result in a psychotic episode. This phenomenon is often portrayed in their artwork by the appearance of black holes in many sizes and forms and by showing themselves falling into a bottomless black pit. These particular patients are sufficiently in touch with reality to observe their own potential psychosis. Since this terror is enormous, they feel safer when they have structure. The pictorialization of their fears helps the art therapist to provide symbolic containment in the session.

Ogden (1989) emphasizes the importance of sensory impressions, particularly at the skin surface, during the earliest stages of life. These impressions become the principal media for the creation of psychological meaning and the rudiments of the experience of self. Object relationships of sensory contiguity over time generate the sense of a bounded sensory surface upon which one's experience occurs. If this is impaired, a unique form of anxiety arises, which Ogden describes as the terror over the prospect that the boundedness of one's sensory surface might be dissolved, with a resultant feeling of falling, leaking, dropping into an endless and shapeless space. Anzieu (1989) further elaborates the importance of this phenomenon in a theory of the "skin-ego." Just as the skin is the envelope to the body, he sees the "skin-ego" as a psychic envelope containing, defining, and protecting the psyche.

The concept of space, of space inside and outside the self, cannot develop unless the containing functions of the skin have been introjected as a result of adequate handling during infancy. Defective skin boundary formation during the stage of adhesive identification (Bick, 1968; Meltzer, 1975) inaugurates the later phenomenon of poverty of ego boundaries, which characterizes psychotic and borderline personalities. A defective boundary between inside and outside may compromise the capacity for reality testing, for which differentiation is necessary. The skin boundary is often perceived as perforated by the borderline patient; it no longer functions as a container. Therefore, it is perceived that intruders can enter, and it results in the flooding out of internal contents. The term "semipermeable membrane" has been used by both patients and clinicians to describe this phenomenon. One patient attempted to portray this permeability by using scissors to cut many little holes and by making small dots on a piece of paper. The holes and dots were her attempt to communicate the experience of not being able to "keep anything inside." She claimed, "I feel void and empty all of the time."

In this light, their weakened, thin, and irregular skin boundaries are responsible for borderline patients' commonly expressed feelings of transparency and corresponding shame and embarrassment. The drawing entitled "Shame" is a patient's portrayal of her feelings of transparency (Figure 4.3). Her fear of being "known" was so great that she had no ability to protect herself. The feeling of

Figure 4.3.   Shame

Figure 4.4.   Safety, maybe

being unable to ward off stares from the outside world is represented by ar-rows. This person needed to enclose herself in a series of symbolically drawn boundaries, which also served to keep her shameful contents inside. The phenomenon of protecting dangerous internal material often manifests itself in paranoid ideation and in the need to stay isolated.

A paranoid psychotic episode was brought on by a patient's drug binge that occurred when his girlfriend left him. During the first few months of his hospitalization, this young man was almost nonverbal, spending most of his time in his room drawing or daydreaming. As his art psychotherapist, I was the only person he would talk to, albeit minimally at first. He would communicate only through his pictures, since this was the way he felt most understood (Figure 4.4). Of significance in this drawing is the appearance of the "eyes," which are commonly seen when paranoid ideation is experienced. Also of note is the "glass dome" in which he "encapsulated" himself for protection. The rigid style of the image, reflecting his attempt to contain and control his own process, is further demonstrated in the excessive outlining of every aspect of the picture, even the shadows.

Dozens of "monsters" with enormous eyes were created by a female patient who represented a hallucination that she saw in the mirror (Figure 4.5). This woman believed that she was being watched by cruel, penetrating, inhuman, inescapable eyes. Her anticipation of the persecution of these all-seeing eyes was pervasive; these eyes could preceive her degradation and humiliation. When the patient made these drawings, she was demonstrating a pronounced

Figure 4.5. The monster in the mirror

loss of interest in the external world. She became silent, seldom left her room, and often scratched her arms with sharp objects. The absence of a mouth is symbolic of her silence, and the blood dripping from the claws of some of these monster images delineates her self-mutilation. The wish to avoid persecution also drove the patient to recurring episodes of panic and rage. She ran away in desperate attempts to escape, and struck out at hospital staff with biting sarcasm and verbal abuse. In addition, the patient resorted to the use of drugs in an effort to obliterate her awareness of the attacking forces within her mind. It is noteworthy that most of the eyes of her monsters appear as large black holes.

"Picture of My Deformity" is another illustration of the poverty of skin and ego boundaries done by a young female patient (Figure 4.6). An attempt to draw the human form reveals the contents of the body. The "X-ray" phenomenon is very common in the artwork of schizophrenic patients and is evidence of the psychotic part (weakened ego/skin boundaries) of this patient's personality. The patient, who was hospitalized for major depression, heroin abuse, and suicide threats, was making an attempt to portray her "defect." "It runs all through my mind and body. . . . I feel like an empty, rotting shell . . . yet it still has a heart and is alive, but sad." Besides the sad, wanton expression on the face, the cagelike

Figure 4.6.   Picture of my deformity

appearance of the lines over the breasts and heart reflect the unavailability of nurturance. Also evident in the drawing is an emphasis upon the intestines, undoubtedly because the patient often suffered from colitis. Her inability to nurture and soothe herself is evident, as well as the rapidity with which she must get rid of anything put inside of her. She was unable to contain or utilize "good food."

Self-mutilation often emanates from a desire to "cut out the bad parts of the self," to "penetrate the deadness," or reaffirm the presence of a skin boundary. It is also an attempt to substitute physical pain for emotional pain, which is more frightening and excruciating. One patient was able to substitute making a damaging picture for doing damage to her own body; she entitled the effort "Drain the Pain," which portrayed a knife imbedded in her head, cuts on her wrist, and blood pouring profusely from these wounds. Encouragement of this act of symbolically putting self-destructive impulses onto the paper in art therapy sessions allowed the patient to discharge those impulses and to convey the enormity of her psychic pain. Because it became a shared experience between patient and therapist, the illustration of the pain brought a sense of relief. Sharing the pain diminished the need to enter into a dissociative state of deadness. The repeated creation of artwork that contained self-mutilation facilitated the cessation of this acting-out behavior.

Adler (1985) theorizes that borderlines suffer from a profound dread of annihilation as the result of separation. He describes the borderline personality as exquisitely vulnerable to any stress arising within a dyadic situation and highly prone to regression in all areas of ego functioning, object relations, and self-cohesiveness. He suggests that borderline individuals suffer from a developmental failure in the formation of introjects, which ordinarily provide the self with the security of holding and soothing.

The fear of abandonment is paramount for the borderline patient. It includes a growing sense of inner emptiness, impairment of object constancy, and a decrease in the capacity to modulate affect, often resulting in rage reactions. The deeper the regression, the greater likelihood that primary process thinking will emerge, leading to possible transient psychotic episodes and an intensification of the subjective sense of nothingness. The rage and fear may take hold to such an extent that the patient suffers annihilation panic, the feeling that the self is very near to disintegration (Adler 1985). Annihilation panic is based on a relative absence of positive introjects around which the self can organize. Borderline patients, therefore, depend upon external objects to keep the fears of annihilation at a tolerable level.

A patient represented her feeling of being left when her therapist went on vacation by painting a large black balloon surrounded by many arrows. As a caption she wrote, "Being abandoned is like being a black balloon that everyone is puncturing so I am left bleeding and deflated." Here again there is the use of the black hole as a metaphor for the void, the emptiness, and the terror of dissolution.

THE PSYCHOTIC TWIN: A CASE STUDY

Peter was a 31-year-old man who was hospitalized over a period of 18 months for depressive episodes, suicidal ideation, and multiple substance abuse. He presented himself as a calm yet highly guarded and suspicious young man. The patient presented with feelings of hopelessness, helplessness, worthlessness, and loneliness. These states were accompanied by episodes of paralyzing anxiety, suicidal rumination, paranoid ideation, and uncontrollable anger.

During brief psychotic episodes, Peter suffered from severe persecutory terror, especially at night. He had auditory hallucinations and a preoccupation with body disintegration. He reported pervasive feelings of confusion. During his psychotic periods his substance abuse increased dramatically, especially when he was overwhelmed by a sense of internal emptiness, loss, and vengeful rage. The diagnostic impression given upon admission was borderline personality disorder with depressive and paranoid features: schizophrenic reaction, schizoaffective type.

Peter was raised by an alcoholic mother and stepfather who abused him physically and mentally. He also reported being sexually molested by a priest as a young child. His adolescence was dominated by drug abuse and minor delinquent activities. The patient was in the military service in Vietnam and was dishonorably discharged because of "incorrigible behavior" and conflict with his superiors. Peter never married and his relationships with women were generally superficial, of short duration, and primarily sexual. The most recent one was filled with tension due to the conflict between his idealization of women and his contempt for them. In his relationships he was very dependent and pervasively depressed. The possibility of intimacy always evoked tremendous panic and personality disintegration. The closer he felt in a relationship, the greater his confusion and fantasies of merger would become. It would evolve to the point at which he was unable to distinguish his own thoughts from those of the other person.

Peter had a strong, almost frightening, effect upon people in his vicinity. His affect was usually constricted, his face in a near-frozen state. Peter's eyes, which were set in an intense stare, reflected both his own terror and a cold hostility. His powerful and engaging presence guaranteed that his entrance into a room was always noticed. Most of the other patients on the ward were frightened of him, although he appeared essentially "normal." Peter's physical attractiveness initially drew people to him, but it belied his underlying rage, terror, and diffusion. That he radiated both power and alienation only heightened this young man's isolation and loneliness. Clinical art therapy sessions with Peter were often difficult, because he evoked intense countertransference responses.

The images Peter produced during the initial phases of treatment were similar to those of psychotic patients in both form and content; they were typical of schizophrenic drawing. He showed marked disintegration of spatial organization and fragmentation, as the figures were not integrated into a cohesive whole human form. Body parts were misplaced, directionality was inconsistent, and there was as an absence of clear body-boundary lines. This is evidenced in Figure 4.7, and in a self-portrait, which he entitled "Despair." Both convey the intense pain of hopelessness and the lack of a cohesive self. When Peter's treatment began, he had tremendous difficulty expressing himself verbally. His speech was slow, barely audible, and lacked spontaneity. His mouth often twitched, which caused him to talk hesitantly in a near-stutter.

After an initial phase of resistance to the art modality, Peter became involved in the process and welcomed every opportunity to draw. In addition to our biweekly sessions, Peter drew on his own time and brought his work into the sessions. As he began to regard his art productions more closely, he was able to observe how "crazy" they appeared, and he recognized his need for ongoing treatment. In the past, he had been unable to make such a commitment and had frequently withdrawn from psychotherapy.

As work progressed, the "twin" parts of Peter's personality became more apparent. His drawings of two figures superimposed one upon the other portray his dual nature. The frequent appearance of double images in his

Figure 4.7.   Psychotic disorganization

Figure 4.8. Confusion

artwork embodied his wish to merge. When Peter became more aware of the traumatic absence of constant nurturing in his early life, he produced a drawing of a self-portrait facing a breast, which reflected his confusion, rage, and painful loneliness (Figure 4.8). While he was drawing the breast with the nipple on it, his affect began to soften, his eyes filled up with tears, and he said, "I have no idea what this means . . . all of a sudden I got very sad." It became clear to both of us that he felt deprived of something very important. My presence as a female therapist became a vital component of the transference at that point in the treatment.

The breast and the human form became the central focus of many of his drawings for months of treatment. These symbols underwent many changes and distortions, reflecting the continuation of an unconscious working-through process. Peter's art illustrates the evolution of these forms at a psychotic level. Throughout the main period of his treatment, there was a feminine appearance to all of his self-portraits, and many of his human forms were an amorphous mixture of both genders. The unconscious, fantasized fusion with the breast led to confusion of sexual identification on an unconscious level. The combination of feminine facial features with male genitals and the further psychotic decompensation of the body into an angular, distorted shape without hands or feet illustrate Peter's confusion (Figure 4.9). At this time, the appearance of the bird and the breast became an integral theme in the unconscious drama of the treatment.

Figure 4.9.   The bird, the breast and gender confusion

Peter was sexually promiscuous, including many of the female patients on the ward in his seductions. In his merger with the female on an unconscious level, she became an object of both desire and hatred, reflecting the defective splitting process in the early symbiotic phase of development. His envy of the female (breast) caused him to distort the female image into something danger-ous and ugly. As he projected his rage into it, the breast became a persecutor that could attack and harm him (Klein, 1975). These dynamics were also evident in the transference. Peter included pointed breasts and genitals on an already distorted form (Figure 4.10). In fact, one breast is pointed and the other rounded, possibly suggestive of the "good breast-bad breast" split, a theme that appeared in other drawings. The image on the left side of the picture portrays a transformation of the breast wherein the nipple gradually becomes the sharp, biting beak of a bird. In the lower right corner there is an infant, lying passively with his mind x-ed out. It appears as though the x's on and surrounding the breast/bird have been placed upon the head of the baby.

Many of the same elements are present in another drawing, "Torn Apart," (Figure 4.11) in which the nipples of the breasts that form the shape of the human figure are colored in red, indicating the intensity of the depicted pain. The nipples are bleeding, and drops of blood are falling from the beak of the bird/breast, again indicating vicious, envious attacks upon the good breasts. A new element, a cluster of circles, appears in the upper righthand corner, herald-

Figure 4.10.   The persecuting breast

Figure 4.11.   Torn apart

ing the beginning of a new symbol. It represents the onset of the organization of all the chaotic and painful thoughts, the development of a more cohesive self. Peter labeled this symbol "Some Support."

The notable improvement in Peter's self-portrait is representative of the gradual process of integration (Figure 4.12). The verbal content of his sessions at this time often focused on his idealized transferences in his relationships with both his psychiatrist and this author. In reference to this alliance, in one of his pictures he portrayed a frightened little boy running back and forth between two good breasts. He was gradually able to perceive the art therapist as the ideal nurturing female, who not only provided him with the food of empathy and understanding, but also acted as a container for all of his rage, despair, and psychotic confusion. It took him many months of work and testing to overcome the fear that his rage would ultimately destroy this significant, safe relationship.

As Peter became more integrated, he was able to utilize his observing ego more often. He attempted to understand the process of art therapy and the role of interpretation in his treatment. His effort to organize what had formerly been chaotic was evidenced in his artwork, in which he utilized small compartments drawn in the place of his brain to identify specific affects. This became a technique that Peter used to keep his thoughts organized and to diminish episodes of confusion.

During the course of treatment, Peter was able to increase his ability to differentiate reality from fantasy. His verbalization became clearer, more coherent,

Figure 4.12.   Self-portrait of Peter

Figure 4.13.   This is me.

with no overt evidence of loosened association. The art therapy played a major role in enabling him to understand his own dynamic process and in decreasing his level of defensive denial. The grip of the primitive defense mechanisms of splitting and projective identification also lessened. At termination, he was better able to identify affects, without being overwhelmed by rage. He was brought to a point of acknowledging his experience of emptiness and his lack of a core self. Peter, through his graphic productions, learned to communicate the psychological catastrophe he felt to be at the foundation of his being. Just prior to his discharge from the hospital, Peter pictorially recorded a remarkable increase in self-cohesiveness in the pictured improvement in his body image entitled, "This is Me" (Figure 4.13).

IMPLICATIONS FOR TREATMENT

Art Therapy: A Symbolic Holding Environment

In my experience as an art psychotherapist in a psychiatric hospital, border-line patients, in particular, approach art therapy with remarkable enthusiasm, both on an individual basis and in group. They often state that they feel "understood" and declare their emotional relief.

Bion (1967) states in his Preface to *Second Thoughts*, "Memory is born of and only suited to sensuous experience" (p. 1). Perhaps *the pictorial representation of an internal experience is a more accurate recreation of unconscious sense experience than can be achieved in words alone.* Sensory experiences are *infra-verbal,* that is, below, beneath, or before language.

Graphic images are representational communication in pictorial form, and at the same time, a *process* by which undifferentiated, disorganized thoughts can be symbolically *contained* and *controlled.* Since many borderline patients have difficulty with symbol formation and abstract thinking, working in *concrete* pictorial symbols can serve a valuable function. Drawings of fragmented and disorganized images can be reduced to segments or compartments as a way to clarify and manage thinking.

Through art, a patient can symbolically control the dangerous experiences of fragmentation. A strong outline that compensates for weakened ego boundaries is a common feature of the artwork of borderline patients. Such encapsulation in graphic images functions as a protective maneuver by avoiding impingement from the outside, or total loss of fragmented parts of the self. One patient described it by saying, "Hold the pieces . . . don't let the outside edge go away" (Figure 4.14). An important indicator of a patient's progression or regression in treatment is the appearance and disappearance of boundary lines. Encapsulation is evident in the drawing of a young man, hospitalized after a severe episode of paranoid psychosis. He attempted to outline everything in the drawing, keeping all elements of the graphic representation separate, even shadows. The encapsulations in his drawing were his way of protecting himself from the confusion inside and from the external impingement his weakened ego boundaries would permit if he reduced his rigidity.

Borderline patients vividly talk about their longing to be held and contained and about their panic about being dropped, abandoned, or rejected. Especially during an episode of psychotic regression, when the patient is experiencing his or her greatest fragmentation, a borderline patient is most in need of containment, "good enough mothering," and a "holding environment" (Winnicott, 1971). The "abandoned-child" feelings of the enraged, regressed borderline patient are accompanied by distrust, panic, and a feeling of being unsupported. A transient loss of memory for important, sustaining people contributes significantly to feelings of being forsaken and isolated (Adler, 1985).

Art therapy techniques can provide the containing, holding environment. Both the therapist and the paper itself help to contain frightening feelings. The art materials serve as tools for the exploration and understanding of powerful emotions. The art therapy environment is a "safe" place where the patient can gain the object distance that encourages insight.

There are certain occasions when the practitioner draws on the same paper as the patient, either simultaneously or alternately. The therapist can thus become the "good enough mother" through having access to the patient's

Figure 4.14.   "Don't let the outside edge go away!"

terrifying internal state, a state that is probably based more on sensations than on words. The therapist can, therefore, respond with the empathic understanding necessary to make the therapeutic work meaningful.

This conjoint work parallels the process Bion (1962) termed *alpha* function. It is the mother's ability to apply words and meaning to the infant's behavior and internal experiences. In other words, the mother/therapist, within her capacity for "reverie," receives and withstands the intolerable, confusing sensations and affect of her child/patient and returns effective, meaningful communication.

More specifically, the therapist's direct involvement becomes a transitional phenomenon that supports the development of a sense of selfhood. Winnicott (1953, 1971; Davis & Wallbridge, 1981), in discussing his theory of play, describes a "potential space" that exists between mother and baby. Within this space a play experience occurs that leads significantly to the formation of the infant's identity. In the "potential space" the creative play arises in which the use of symbols develops. The use of symbols is a way of being in touch with the inner psychic reality, that is, of discovering the self. It is what Winnicott calls "creative apperception," which happens when the baby first looks into his mother's eyes; because he discovers himself there, he also begins to discover meaning in the world. Meaning becomes attached to "transitional phenomena," and then to playing and to living creatively. The loss of play, which can come about through deprivation, includes the loss of the symbol. The self-discovery that Winnicott describes as taking place in the "potential space" is the same as the realization of individual potential.

It follows, therefore, that art therapy can replicate this "potential space." The ability to form and use symbols brings meaning to the world of shared reality. Since many borderline patients lack the capacity for the spontaneous, creative use of symbols, the art therapy process can be especially helpful for them. More specifically, the art therapist's *direct* involvement becomes a "transitional phenomenon" in this "potential space" that supports the development of a sense of selfhood.

A blank sheet of paper, symbolically analogous to time and space in life, can be very frightening to an individual who is already filled with intense fear and aloneness. Initially, it can represent the endless void dreaded by the patient who is on the edge of, or in the midst of, a psychotic episode. A simple mark, a line, or a squiggle made by the therapist provides a point of contact. It introduces structure, with which the patient can connect visually. The patient may respond through graphic communication, either by completing the picture alone or by drawing alternately with the therapist. With hospitalized borderline patients, in particular, this process has often aided a patient in making thoughts and feelings available for meaningful therapeutic work. Because it is conducive to the differentiation of self and "not-self," creating art helps the patient feel less alone and better contained.

Searles (1982) describes a striking loss of memory for childhood events as a typical feature of borderline patients. He proposes that this amnesia serves as an unconscious defense against all types of negative emotions, guilt, fear, shame, and grief. Since the strong negative feelings include rage of enormous proportions, childhood amnesia circumvents murderous feelings. When the events are painful or unpleasurable, the individual's impulse is to evacuate such elements. Borderline individuals often "murder" large periods of their past or important people in their lives, especially family members. Art therapy in general, and dyadic art in particular, lead to the revival of significant memories, both positive and negative. Memories are, most probably, stored as images (or sensory traces) in the unconscious mind. When an image is perceived, it impacts both the conscious and the unconscious and thereby evokes a retrieval process of a long-forgotten memory by identification with a similar image (or sensory experience). The following case material illustrates the role of art therapy in regard to amnesia or repressed material.

Jane, a 33-year-old woman, had been raped several times during adolescence and young adulthood and possibly molested by a brother when she was a child. She has totally blocked all memory of the assaults until she produced a series of drawings made in response to my original mark on the paper. The first picture was an image of a person on her knees, bent over a knife and a pool of blood. The next item in the series showed her screaming "No!" to her attacker. In the last drawing, a looping line I drew became suggestive of her buttocks and anus, representing an anal rape and knife cuts. When Jane produced the last pictures, tears flooded her eyes and she voiced her shock, shame, and rage at the recollection of these traumas.

During the several succeeding sessions, Jane was practically mute. Angry and frightened, she was terrified by her contact with these memories and by her feelings of vulnerability and rage. She expressed a fear of "totally falling apart and never being able to put all (her) pieces together, ever again!"

The recollection of these traumatic events provided important information for Jane's overall treatment. The therapy also gave her a safe "holding environment" where she found herself able to express the terror and humiliation that had been repressed in the past. Through her drawings and through the reestablishment of verbal communication, Jane was able to understand the continual sensations of vulnerability and danger she experienced in her early years due to the absence of a sustained, contained, holding environment.

The Circle as a Holding Method: Case Histories

A circle drawn by the therapist can provide a patient with the special feelings of being held and enveloped. It can become a focused area where scattered, fragmented thoughts and frightening sensation-images can be placed. The therapist establishes a boundary that is round and has no sharp edges, points, or corners. The approach of drawing a circle is effective when a patient is feeling frightened of going out of control. When the drawing or design within the circle is completed, patients usually appear calmer and report feeling more centered, relaxed, and safe.

Caroline, an immature 20-year-old woman, was seen in individual art psychotherapy twice a week for a period of 18 months. She was hospitalized during an episode of psychotic decompensation, marked by confusion, fragmentation, and the alternation of emotional lability with periods of affectlessness. When she believed herself to be emotionally "dead," Caroline would scrape or scratch herself until she bled, claiming that she never felt the pain.

At the beginning of treatment, Caroline suffered greatly due to episodes of intense mental confusion. She would pace about the room, highly agitated, holding her head and in tears would cry out, "I'm so scared. . . . What is happening to me! . . . My brain hurts!" In a collage produced during her first art therapy session, she depicted her emotional pain and confusion. In her selection of magazine photos, she represented the internal anguish she was unable to verbalize. The artwork clearly conveyed the overwhelming panic of the child about to be abandoned. Caroline produced this art during a nonverbal period when she was unable to otherwise convey her terror and loss of control resulting from the unbearable pain of loss. The paper upon which pictures were pasted served as a container for overwhelming emotions. The images were glued down in a rapid and disorganized fashion. The principal colors were red and black, and she filled in all of the white spaces between the photos with a red marker, suggesting her pain and rage. Caroline cried while she worked, but she did not speak.

In one of the sessions, the patient became agitated and cried. She was given a sheet of paper upon which was drawn a circle with a point in the center. Caroline, with some difficulty, drew within the circle. During the next several months, she completed many such drawings, utilizing a circle as a center point upon which she would organize her disordered thought processes (Figure 4.15). She completed a large number of similar designs during her 18 months of hospitalized treatment.

Caroline's designs illustrate how her reorganization evolved over a period of time. They progressed in their degree of structure, as well as in their use of abstract images, symbolizing the core issues she focused upon in her treatment. The patient often declared her feelings of tremendous "relief" when she finished the artwork. She appeared calmer and less panicked. When she had episodes of frightening psychotic anxiety, she would ask for extra pieces of paper with circles drawn upon them to work on independently between our sessions. Caroline used this contained space not only to evacuate her "crazy" thoughts, but also to reorganize them into meaningful symbolic images. The work with the circles led to her development of an observing ego, which in turn enabled her to exercise control over her internal chaos. With the support of the art therapist's interpretations, she was helped to understand her symbolic communication and made remarkable progress. Two of her final designs, drawn during the termination phase of her treatment, reveal her success with increased structure and focus (Figure 4.16, p. 106).

The circle drawing technique was used with another hospitalized patient named Roberta, during her periods of decompensation. Being very frightened of weakening ego boundaries and dissolution, Roberta was too terrified to draw alone and needed my direct involvement. Therefore, during the early phase of treatment we created conjoint drawings.

Roberta would ask me to draw heavy black lines inside the circle for her. She would then reinforce the form with a black pastel or marker. We simultaneously proceeded to fill it in with colors of her choosing. Each color had a symbolic meaning, which she indicated were the different parts of herself, myself, and her analyst. As a result, the colors tended to soothe her.

One day, when she was particularly distraught, Roberta and I drew in pale blue, lavender, and pink. Tears fell gently down her cheeks while we worked quietly together. Upon completion of a design contained within a circle, she asked me to write the following on the back of the page:

I need to find a quiet place that is comfortable and soothing. I need Diane to write it down so I will have a sense of her being in there with me. It is a

Figure 4.15.   The holding circle

Figure 4.16.   The holding circle: increased structure and form

different way of not being alone and being comforted. I created this place myself and worked at it until I felt comfortable. Diane . . . gave me permission by making me feel safe enough. I felt held enough.

The artwork entitled "Feeling Fragmented and Need Sorting Out" (Figure 4.17, p. 108), illustrates how Roberta used this method effectively. This patient used obsessive control to manage her states of panic. She associated the following with her pictures:

> . . . I struggle with . . . the fear of being out of control . . . then I become boxed in . . . too tight, can't move at all. . . . I prefer movement drawings, but I am scared of moving in space because I get all out of control.

Roberta believed it to be very important that the final product was filled in solidly. She insisted that not even one speck of white paper be allowed to show through. As therapy progressed, she was better able to do an entire drawing herself, without needing to draw upon the additional ego strength provided by the therapist in the dual drawings. Through a slow process she also eventually relinquished the intense black outlines. Finally, Roberta let go of the circle altogether and used the entire sheet of paper. Her autonomy and ability to self-soothe had grown to the point of no longer needing the containment they provided.

CONCLUDING REMARKS

Borderline patients are often flooded by many thoughts that cause them considerable distress. Because they have difficulty in both thinking and talking, they become overstimulated and overwhelmed and are not able to encode and order their thoughts effectively. The graphic representation of their experiences can help them to sort through the chaos, giving them a sense of relief. The artwork helps these individuals develop the ability to "think the thought," as Bion (1963) phrased it. The concrete, graphic representation of images and emotions makes it easier to label internal states, rather than drifting in a world of sensation-dominated impulses.

Entering the internal world of the borderline patient through art psychotherapy permits the creation of a holding, containing environment where the development of meaning can take place. Through deep understanding, empathy, and interpretation, the art therapist can contribute to the creation of a solid, secure self-image as well as significant and healthy bonding with others.

Figure 4.17.   "Feeling fragmented and need sorting out"

REFERENCES

Adler, G. (1985). *Borderline Psychopathology and Its Treatment*. New York: Jason Aronson.

Adler, G., & Buie, D. (1979). Psychotherapeutic approach to aloneness in the borderline patient. In Le Boit & Capponi (Eds.), *Advances in Psychotherapy of the Borderline Patient*. New York: Jason Aronson.

Anzieu, D. (1989). *The Skin Ego*. New Haven: Yale University Press.

Bick, E. (1968). Experience of the skin in early object relations. *International Journal of Psychoanalysis, 49,* 484–486.

Bion, W. (1962). *Learning from Experience*. London: Heinemann.

Bion, W. (1963). *Elements of Psychoanalysis*. London: Heinemann.

Bion, W. (1967). *Second Thoughts*. London: Maresfield Reprints.

Davis, M., & Wallbridge, D. (1981). *Boundary and Space: An Introduction to the Work of D. W. Winnicott*. New York: Brunner/Mazel.

Eigen, M. (1986). *The Psychotic Core*. Northvale, NJ: Jason Aronson.

Grotstein, J. S. (1979). The psychoanalytic concept of the borderline organization. In LeBoit & Capponi (Eds.), *Advances in Psychotherapy of the Borderline Patient*. New York: Jason Aronson.

Grotstein, J. S. (1982). The analysis of a borderline patient. In P. Giovacchini & B. Boyer (Eds.), *Technical Factors in the Treatment of the Severely Disturbed Patient*. New York: Jason Aronson.

Grotstein, J. S. (1983). A proposed revision of the psychoanalytic concept of primitive mental states, Part 2. The borderline syndrome—Section I. Disorders of autistic safety and symbiotic relatedness. *Contemporary Psychoanalysis, 19*(4), 570–604.

Grotstein, J. S. (1984a). A proposed revision of the psychoanalytic concept of primitive mental states, Part 2. The borderline syndrome—Section 2. The phenomenology of the borderline syndrome. *Contemporary Psychoanalysis, 20*(1), 77–119.

Grotstein, J. S. (1984b). A proposed revision of the psychoanalytic concept of primitive mental states, Part 2. The borderline syndrome—Section 3. Disorders of autistic safety and symbiotic relatedness. *Contemporary Psychoanalysis, 20*(2), 266–343.

Klein, M. (1975). *Envy and Gratitude*. England: Hogarth Press.

Masterson, J. (1976). *Psychotherapy of the Borderline Adult: A Developmental Approach*. New York: Brunner/Mazel.

Masterson, J. (1981). *The Narcissistic and Borderline Disorders: An Integrated Developmental Approach*. New York: Brunner/Mazel.

Meltzer, D. (1975). Adhesive Identification. *Contemporary Psychoanalysis, 11,* 289–310.

Ogden, T. (1989). *The Primitive Edge of Experience*. Northvale, NJ: Jason Aronson.

Piaget, J. (1962). *Play, Dreams and Imitation in Childhood*. New York: Norton.

Searles, H. (1982). Some aspects of separation and loss in psychoanalytic therapy with borderline patients. In P. Giovacchini & B. Boyer (Eds.), *Technical Factors in the Treatment of the Severely Disturbed Patient*. New York: Jason Aronson.

Tustin, F. (1981). *Autistic States in Children.* London: Routledge and Kegan Paul.
Winnicott, D. W. (1953). Transitional objects and transitional phenomena. *International Journal of PsychoAnalysis. 34,* 89–97.
Winnicott, D. W. (1971). *Playing and Reality.* London and New York: Tavistock Publications.

Chapter 5

Mothers of Incestuously Abused Children in Group Art Therapy

Sandra Stark Shields

Modern, rigorously controlled studies have uncovered ever increasing numbers of sexually abused victims. In a study conducted by Russell (1983) on the incidence of intrafamilial and extrafamilial sexual abuse of female children, 16 percent of the women surveyed reported having had at least one exploitative intrafamilial sexual contact prior to age 18. Another researcher, Finkelhor (1980), surveyed college students in New England. On the basis of his study, he concluded that one in every 100 adult women in the United States was sexually molested by her father in childhood. Despite a growing awareness of the problem, most clinicians believe that the incidence of incest and sexual abuse is much higher than reported in the literature because the average child may never disclose the secret (Press, Morris, & Sandza, 1981; Summit, 1983). In their text, Hillman and Solek-Tefft (1988) comment, "Child sexual abuse is perhaps the most unreported crime in the country at this time" (p. 1).

The psychological literature typically portrays the mother in incestuous families in a negative light. Some researchers state that the mother knows about the incest at some level of consciousness or actively "sets up" the incestuous relationship. Other authors cite personality characteristics or actions taken by the mother that may help to facilitate the sexual abuse (Herman, 1983; Justice & Justice, 1979; Lustig, Dresser, Spellman, & Murry, 1966; Selby, Calhoun, Jones, & Matthews, 1980; Sgroi, 1982; Zuelzer & Reposa, 1983).

There are also researchers who see the mother as a victim rather than as a coconspirator. They underscore such contributing factors as abandonment and/or sexual abuse during childhood, repetitive physical abuse by the spouse, and society's traditional patriarchal norms (Goodwin, McCarty, & DiVasto, 1981; Gordy, 1983; McIntyre, 1981; Prince, 1981; Summit, 1983; Taubman, 1984).

Whatever the factors were that influenced the mother's role in the incestuous family, blaming the mother for her collusion during treatment is decidedly antitherapeutic (Dietz & Craft, 1980). Instead, vigorous outreach and immediate support that "feels like help" is needed to keep these often isolated and fearful women in treatment (Sgroi, 1982). Effective treatment becomes mandatory, given the mother's important role of informing the authorities about the sexual abuse, protecting her children, enforcing boundaries, and changing communication patterns in the family.

PROFILE OF THE VICTIM'S MOTHER

A negative view of the mother's personality is seen in a survey conducted by Selby, Calhoun, Jones, and Matthews (1980), who found that 50 percent of the social workers they polled described these women as quiet, submissive, passive, and remote. In addition, 85 percent of the social workers stated that the mothers had "pretended not to know" about the incest relationship between father and daughter. Dietz and Craft (1980) also surveyed protective service workers and found that when the worker saw the mother as "to blame" or as "colluding" with the incestuous abuse, they were less likely to assess whether or not the mother was herself the victim of wife battering.

Sgroi (1982) points out that mothers in incestuous families tend to be "psychologically absent" in their relationships with both husband and children. Often a lack of psychological investment can be seen in the interpersonal aspects of their marriage and family lives. Sgroi lists a number of personality traits and treatment issues of mothers in incestuous families, which she used to formulate an intervention plan:

1. Inability to trust others because of past betrayals;
2. Impaired self-image marked by feelings of low self-esteem, limited knowledge of emotional states, and poor awareness of their own sexuality;
3. Denial of feelings and denial that the sexual abuse occurred;
4. Unreasonable expectations of appropriate roles and responsibilities of family members;
5. Failure to establish and enforce behavioral limits and family boundaries;
6. Pent-up anger at their family of origin, their present family, and "the system";
7. Poor family communication;
8. Lack of assertiveness about meeting their own needs in the family;
9. Poor social skills and isolation;
10. Need for help with "practical" issues such as the social service and court systems, public assistance, household management, and parenting skills.

In her article "Recognition and Treatment of Incestuous Families," Herman (1983) discusses the presence of a "disability" among mothers in incestuous families. She notes that it is not unusual for the mother not to drive a car. In addition, the mother seems barely able to take care of herself and her children. Undiagnosed major mental illnesses such as schizophrenia, depression, alcoholism, and frequent pregnancies are also included as impairments. Herman also points out that the husband does not assume a maternal role when the mother is disabled; rather, the oldest daughter takes on the caretaking role. A sexual relationship with the father then becomes an extension of the daughter's other duties. Role reversal between mother and daughter is also discussed by Lustig et al. (1966) and Will (1983).

Several researchers note a multigenerational "victim-victim" pattern underlying incest. This happens when a female child incest victim who later becomes an adult mother is also unable to protect her own children from the incest-prone men she tends to select (e.g., Goodwin et al., 1981; Sgroi, 1982; Summit, 1983). In the text *Vulnerable Populations* (Sgroi, 1988), Denise Gelinas expands the concept of role-reversal to describe a parentification process, often passed from mother to daughter, whereby the child prematurely takes on excessive caretaking responsibilities for her family. Gelinas goes on to state that if the parentified child does not perform a vital task such as cooking, it simply does not get done.

Dietz and Craft (1980) note the similarities between physically abusive and sexually abusive families. Both kinds of families are presented as patriarchal, with dominant husbands and submissive wives. In both instances the father typically underscores his position with drinking, violence, bribes, and restrictions on the social lives of family members. Dietz and Craft state that the similarities between these two types of families suggest there is often wife battering in incestuous families as well.

The presence of physical abuse led Dietz and Craft to take a different view of the mothers. Instead of seeing these women as having colluded with the incest, they see the mothers' lack of action to protect their children or leave the incestuous family as similar to the behavior of mothers in physically abusive families. Thus, mothers in both situations may be afraid to report the abuse because of: (a) fear of violent physical retaliation by their husbands; (b) lack of a safe refuge for themselves and their children; (c) an unwillingness or shame about admitting the abuse to outsiders; and (d) a lack of financial or emotional resources to provide for themselves and their children.

Dynamics of the marital relationship are discussed by several researchers. Sgroi (1982) outlines two typical kinds of husband/wife interactions exhibited by incestuous families: the dominant husband or the dependent husband. She notes that wives of dominant husbands tend to be passive women with very low self-esteem and limited social skills, whereas wives of dependent husbands tend to be stronger and more self-assertive with better social skills. Wives of both kinds of husbands tend to be dissatisfied with their marital role and display marked interpersonal and sexual dysfunction. Prince (1981) also discusses the marital relationship in the incestuous family and states that both spouses enter the marriage with histories of problems in their families of origin. Therefore, unmet needs cause both spouses to place excessive demands on each other, while paradoxically pushing one another away due to fears of closeness and poor communication. Thus, incest becomes a way of managing hidden anger, as well as a way to resolve conflicts over closeness and abandonment.

Art therapy literature on the use of this modality to treat adult members of incestuous families is nonexistent. However, several authors have written about the use of art therapy intervention with children who are incest victims (Carozza & Heirsteiner, 1982; Feldman, 1984; Howard & Jakab, 1968; Niatove, 1982).

GROUP ART THERAPY FOR THE MOTHERS OF SEXUALLY ABUSED CHILDREN

The art therapy group described in this chapter was an open, ongoing, long-term support group. The mother's group was part of a sexual abuse treatment program offered by a community outpatient clinic. The meetings were held on a weekly basis for 90 minutes. Eight of these sessions are reported herein.

Group goals included: (1) the members' realization that they were not unique, since they all struggled with the same problem; (b) peer interaction to facilitate the confrontation of incest issues; and (c) aiding the mother to see the child as the victim, rather than the instigator. In addition, my unspoken agenda was to use the art to help group members gain insight into family dynamics and to improve social skills.

Composition of the Group

The group consisted of 14 mothers of incestuously abused children of various ages from various racial and economic backgrounds. Though the average number of mothers in attendance on any given evening was usually eight, the large number of participants, fluctuating attendance, and the introduction of new members adversely affected group cohesion, group process, and participation in the artwork. A closed art therapy group would have been the optimum choice, but this was not possible due to the limited availability of staff for the program.

All of the women and their families were court-ordered into treatment and their cases were supervised by the Department of Children's Services. Eight members had children who participated in children's sexual abuse groups, plus a husband or a boyfriend who was involved in the perpetrator's group. Seven of these women were attempting to reconcile with their partners. Six clients had their children detained in foster placement for a short time after the incest was disclosed, and three had children in long-term foster home placements. Additionally, in a case where a mother and daughter each had abused children in the household, the pair attended these sessions together. This was because another group was not available.

Although six of the participants had already been through the criminal court system, the charges against the perpetrator had been dropped. This situation occurred frequently because the victims either would not or could not testify. In several cases, prosecution was unlikely because of the young ages of their children. The rest of the group members either were in the process of entering the court system or the perpetrator had already been prosecuted.

The group included Dina, an important member who was a six-year veteran of similar therapy groups and who had agreed to participate on a voluntary basis. She often acted as a group catalyst. A social worker from the Department of Children's Services was a cotherapist and frequently provided valuable information on the court and social service systems.

The general mood of the group could best be described as shocked, tearful, overwhelmed, and angry. Although all members were able to share their "story" in time, silences were common. Nonverbal gestures of support were frequently revealed through a look, a sound of disbelief, a touch on the shoulder, or passing the box of Kleenex. The least-common were verbal expressions such as conveying empathy, asking questions, noticing similarities, or confronting behaviors. When these types of verbalizations did occur, they were frequently modeled or elicited by Dina.

The women had difficulty with the verbal interaction aspect of therapy; however, during the creative portion of the session, the mood of the group was generally lighter, sometimes playful. Members usually talked with one another on a social level while working on their pictures. Nevertheless, members hesitated to ask others to pass art materials and were reluctant to share their artwork. This may be connected to the passive role that these women played at home, in addition to poor social skills as recorded by Sgroi (1982). Another reason for low group interaction could also have been due to the initial phase of group development (Yalom, 1975).

The most "curative" part of the group fell under Yalom's concept of "universality." Members frequently made statements such as, "I thought no one would talk to me because I felt like I was wearing a big badge that said 'incest' on it. Now I know that I'm not alone."

There were two art examples done at the beginning of the group, which clearly illustrate the economic and emotional consequences of incest disclosure experienced by most members as they first entered the group. The first was done by Marie in response to a directive that asked members to *utilize magazine collage pictures to describe how their week had been.* Marie selected seven magazine pictures that conveyed an "overwhelmed" impression. Next to the photos of soldiers marching she wrote, "Having to keep in a straight line." An image of eyes meant, "I feel like someone is watching me." Marie stated that both pictures described her experiences with the Department of Children's Services and the threat that her children would again be removed from her home if she did not do as she was told. The client also selected four collage pictures which described her current emotional state. A photo of a rocket represented "I feel like I'm exploding." Under a picture of a woman Marie wrote, "hiding behind sadness." An image of a drain was described with the words "feeling drained," while a cartoon portrayed "feeling like jumping." Last, Marie selected the photograph of a repetitive human outline and wrote, "having to be more than one person" (Figure 5.1). Now that she had to care for her five children alone, Marie talked at length about her struggle to discipline her children, manage the finances, and find some time for herself.

The second art example was produced by Ruby. It depicts the commonly expressed group concern of feeling "boxed in" by the circumstances of their current lives. The picture of a purple catlike figure represents herself and conveys her sense of being surrounded with no means of escape. The artwork opened up a discussion about her fear of her boyfriend (the perpetrator) and the frustration over attempts to get various social service systems involved in her case.

Ruby stated that the large brown circle with the spiked lines that surrounded the catlike figure represented her physically and emotionally abusive boyfriend and her dread of not being able to get away from him. She wrote the words "mask of emotions in/out" and said it referred to her attempt to "pretend that nothing is wrong" in front of her boyfriend (Figure 5.2). She believed that if she confronted him about molesting their two-and-a-half-year-old son without the protection of the social service systems, he would hurt her and try to take her child away. Unfortunately, as is often the case with very young victims, the possibility of criminal court assistance or legal custody action was slim. Thus, Ruby's only option was to protect her son as best she could, alone.

GROUP ART THERAPY SESSIONS

First Session

Theme: Explore and discuss different emotional states.
Art Directives: (1) Select eight emotions as a group; (2) Create a "feelings dictionary"; (3) Select one or two feelings from your dictionary that represent how you are feeling right now.

The literature on mothers of incest victims indicates that low self-esteem is evidenced by a limited awareness of their emotional states. The art directives, as stated above, were used to promote the exploration and differentiation between various feelings.

The therapist began by having the group select eight different emotions to demonstrate how shapes and colors can depict feelings. The women hesitated

Figure 5.1. Overwhelmed

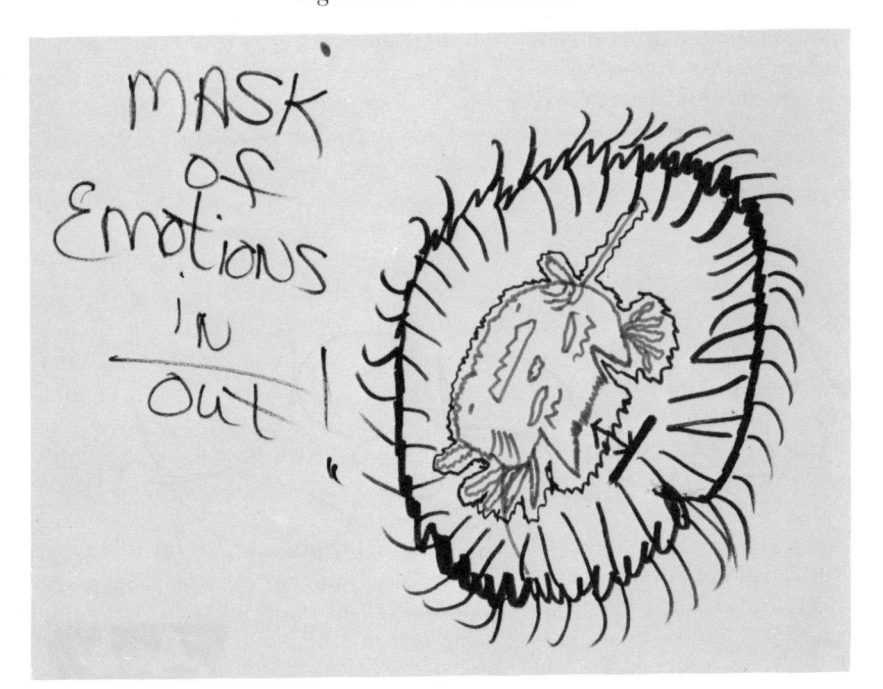

Figure 5.2. Boxed in without escape

at first, asking many questions. They were unsure about the project; nevertheless, they ventured forth to create their art.

The pictures produced in this session contained two different styles, one that was expressive and another that was restrictive. The expressive was marked by the tendency to use distinctly different shapes and colors together with a detailed verbal description of the drawing. The restrictive style contained similarities between shapes and colors, along with an ambiguous and undetailed verbal description. The more assertive group members tended to produce the most expressive dictionaries.

The group members with the more expressive drawings asked to show their work first. Dina, the group member who often acted as a role model, described the meaning of each color and shape in her "feelings dictionary." She used different symbols and colors to distinguish between different emotions. Yet, anger and hate appeared as similarly shaped nonrepresentational scribbles, perhaps indicating a connection between the two feelings. Dina also made large green eyes that conveyed a feeling of frightened surprise, which she labeled "jealousy." The image and word had the potential to evoke feelings inherent in the dynamics of incest. In spite of this fact, none of the group members alluded to such an association. When she was told to depict how she was feeling at the moment, Dina combined the "apathy" and "frustration" symbols to illustrate her feelings about "being in the middle" between various family members during a recent disagreement. The art revealed her passive stance when confronted with a frustrating experience, a feature typical of mothers of victims.

Terri, another highly verbal, sensitive, and often confrontational group member, also produced an expressive "feelings dictionary." Her artwork, like Dina's, also showed similarities between hate and anger by her use of the color black. Of primary interest is the symbol Terri used for "apathy": a blue scribble that she said meant "calm," with dots of black drawn on it to signify occasional moments of anxiety. Several weeks earlier, she had drawn the exact same symbol to portray her ambivalence about reuniting with her boyfriend, the perpetrator. Terri's unconscious replication of this symbol in her "feelings dictionary" to describe "apathy" suggests her struggle in deciding whether or not she should give up the relationship. This issue was often expressed by other women in the group.

Terri's concern about this matter was also seen in her second drawing, where she enlarged the "frustration" symbol and used it to talk about her daughter's "stubbornness" and her disappointment in her boyfriend's lack of participation in treatment.

Ruby's "feelings dictionary" was also of the expressive type. Her symbols and colors were the most diverse and distinctive in the group. Most dramatic is the powerful symbol for "hate," which was drawn as a red, radiating circle. She created "jealousy" as a mother and father on opposite ends pulling at their son who was between them. This drawing reflects her efforts to keep the perpetrating boyfriend away from her son, despite his continued insistence on seeing the

Figure 5.3.   The child in between

child. The "jealousy" picture came the closest to addressing incest issues directly (Figure 5.3).

For the second picture revealing her feelings at the moment, Ruby chose to elaborate on "love." She depicted the wish for a house of her own and a husband who loved her. In the lower lefthand corner, she drew a "husband," a child, and then herself. Once again, in the drawing she placed her child between herself and the wished-for husband. The artwork portrays three interdependent circles encapsulated in the heart, which gives the impression of a desire for fusion.

Joanne, a very quiet person, produced a "feelings dictionary" representative of a more restricted style. Her drawing is devoid of recognizable symbols, and she was unable to explain her choice of colors. Joanne made a large black scribble and used the same shape and color to exhibit both anger and hate (Figure 5.4). To describe her current feelings, she used the anger/hate symbol to show a wish that the perpetrator go to jail for life. The investment and larger size in the anger and hate symbols is also descriptive of Joanne's current emotional crisis.

Figure 5.4.   Anger and hate vented at the perpetrator

Vicki took the longest time to draw her art and was the last member to share it. The small, tightly drawn objects and the lack of color variation are indicative of the restrictive style. Of particular interest to the family dynamics of incest-prone families is the portrayal of "jealousy" as three people sitting on the inside of a triangle. Like the other members who worked within the restrictive style, Vicki provided little verbal description when discussing her picture. Like other participants, she also chose to enlarge the "love" portion of her dictionary.

The tendency of group members to draw anger and hate in a similar manner displays their inability to distinguish between these emotions. This lack of differentiation between feelings seems to have an impact on the appropriate use of anger to "enforce" behavioral limits with their children. Group members admitted having difficulties with setting firm, consistent, behavioral rules with their children for fear of conveying the message "I hate you."

Second Session

Theme: Exploring, recognizing, and discussing the expression of feelings.
Art Directives: (1) Fold your paper in half; (2) On the outside, select pictures that represent feelings that you show to others; (3) On the inside, select pictures that represent feelings that you don't show to others.

The group was apprehensive about the directives and asked the therapist to repeat them a number of times. The concept of inner feelings "not shown to others" was especially confusing and exposed a lack of awareness of an inner emotional life. Group members were also hesitant about disclosing painful feelings.

The content of the pictures ranged from self-disclosing and emotional to those that showed goals instead of feelings.

One of the more revealing pieces of artwork was done by Karen, a very shy member who seldom spoke in group. For her, the art was especially significant, since it helped her to become an active group member. Karen's "outside" collage exhibits the theme of "putting on a front" for others. She picked a photograph of a woman cooking with a look of despair and depression on her face. Since the picture portrays her "outward self," it suggests that she shows her sadness to the family. In addition, the image of a suit of armor with the words "It's all locked in" alludes to the family secret of incest that is kept hidden from others (Figure 5.5).

Figure 5.5. Hiding the family secret

Karen filled the inner emotions portion of the collage with her overwhelmingly sad feelings. On the left side she selected a mother-daughter picture, then drew a tear on the mother's face. She said she wished to take the hurt away from her victimized daughter so they could love each other again. (A poor or disrupted mother-daughter relationship, which is characteristic of incestuously abused children, is poignantly demonstrated by Karen.) On the top right side of the artwork are two photographs of women, one with a suitcase and one with an anguished expression on her face. They represented the feelings of "frustration" about her current family situation and her wish to "tell my family I'm leaving." Beside the image of a man she wrote, "When will it all end?" This desperate question was echoed over and over again by other members of the group. The last collage picture expresses Karen's "loneliness," indicating social isolation and a lack of communication in this woman's family (Figure 5.6).

As previously mentioned, because, at that time, there was only one clinical art therapy group for the mothers whose children were abused, Karen's daughter Marie (see Figure 5.1, p. 117) also attended these sessions. Marie created an evocative collage of a "confident" woman to portray "feelings that she shows to others," adding the words, "Trying to feel good about myself." Like her mother, the "outside" picture also depicts "putting on a front" in public. In contrast, the "inside collage" shows a small, sad figure surrounded by the words that expose

Figure 5.6.   Concealing sad feelings

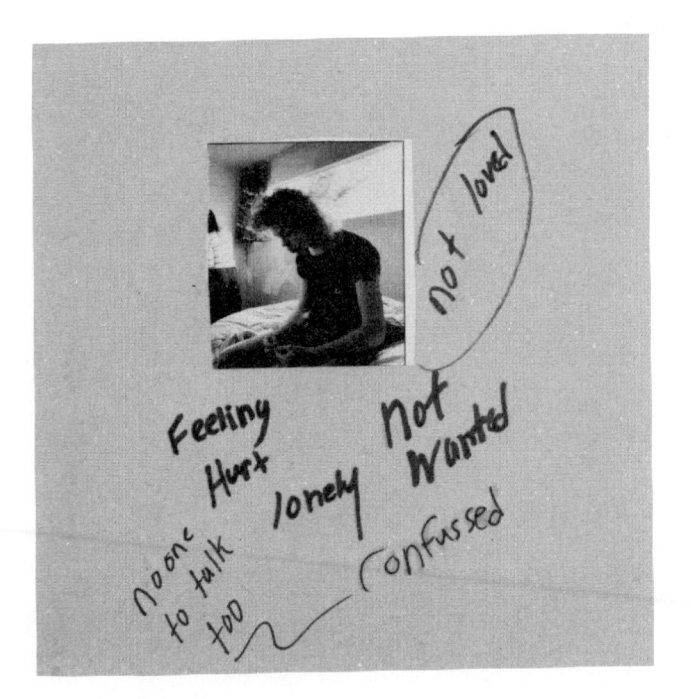

Figure 5.7.   Depression and low self-esteem

her depression, low self-esteem, and loneliness (Figure 5.7). Since this "inside" picture evoked many of the feelings that group members shared, there was a long pause of silent reflection before the group was ready to move on.

The art that had the least to do with emotions and the most to do with goals was done by Vicki. She picked two photos: one of a small woman, which meant people saw her as a nice person; and the other of a group of women, which stood for her wish for more social contacts. Yet, the three women in the photo have menacing, angry facial expressions, indicating Vicki's fears of social relationships and being talked about because of the incest (Figure 5.8). Vicki's "inside" collage contains a photo of a family and another of a person reading a book. This reiterated goals of "getting closer to others" or a desire to "improve myself by taking classes." Although the theme of these pictures points to painful feelings of social and intellectual inadequacy, Vicki managed to avoid any direct depiction of emotions and concentrated instead on goals.

Third Session

Theme: Similarities and differences among family members.
Art Directive: Draw everyone in your family, including yourself, as an animal.

The therapist presented this task as a way of examining the personality traits of family members.

Figure 5.8.   Goals, not emotions

Sarah, a new group member, was very resistant to the exercise and repeatedly claimed that she "couldn't draw." She selected a ballpoint pen and sketched an extremely light picture (darkened here for illustrative purposes). At the beginning of the session, this woman shared her story and stated that she believed her daughter "was not telling the truth about being molested." When other group members asked what she would do if the reports about the molestation of her daughter were true, she admitted that she would be devastated.

Sarah's artwork exhibited her ambivalence about facing the situation. At first, she drew all of her family members, except her oldest daughter, the victim. They were next to each other, lined up across the bottom of the page. The animal figures situated from left to right were: husband as a fox, herself as a stick figure, son as a dog, and the youngest daughter as a cat. Sarah then scribbled over her stick figure, substituting instead a portrayal of herself as a bird flying away from the family. She stated that the bird corresponded to the rage she felt toward her husband and her desire to flee should her daughter's accusations be true. On the upper lefthand side of the paper, Sarah drew her daughter, the victim, as a squirrel next to a tree because she "ran around." Sarah mentioned this child's promiscuity as evidence that her daughter had not been molested. The placement of the abused child outside of the "family line" at the bottom of the page seems representative of the typical family dynamic of scapegoating the victim. This is typical of the "suppression" phase (Sgroi, 1982), and also underscores the reality of her daughter's residency in a foster home. Sarah's final drawing of herself as a bird also illustrates a vicarious identification with her daughter and an effort to believe her accusations (Figure 5.9).

Another new member, Rene, also revealed important family dynamics. She drew her husband and older son as cats, the younger son as a skunk, and herself as a dog. She selected the cat to characterize her husband and older son, because they were "quiet" and "independent," choosing "when" and "if" they wanted to "come to her for affection." She represented her younger son as a skunk because he was "mischievous," and she characterized herself as a "friendly dog." Rene often spoke about her family as if they were still intact, even though both her sons were in permanent foster placement. She and her husband (the perpetrator) had refused to separate so that their sons could be returned to the home. Her tendency to be unrealistic about the family situation indicates her use of denial as a defense.

One of the most colorful pictures was done by Marie. She symbolized her husband as a "grouchy bear" who was largest in size; herself as a pink cat, the same size as the three children on the bottom row; the seven- and five-year-old sons as monkeys who "climb all over things a lot"; a one-year-old son as an otter; the victim, an eight-year-old boy, as a "stinker" skunk; and the nine-year-old daughter, also a victim, as a "happy" rabbit that "bounced around a lot."

The large size of the children on the bottom row of the drawing compared to her portrayal of the two sons on the top row is indicative of the fact that Marie

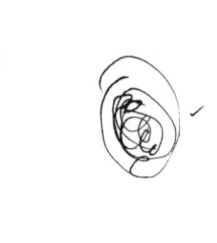

Figure 5.9.　Ambivalent family alliances

Figure 5.10. A wife who is "one of the kids"

put much more time and effort into these offspring. Marie's placement of herself between her husband and her daughter demonstrates her efforts to protect her daughter from further abuse. Last, the contrast between the imposing, dominant bear and the small cat, which is the same size as most of the children, shows that Marie perceived herself as being helpless like her children (Figure 5.10). In fact, she often complained to the group that her husband treated her like "one of the kids," a characteristic of husbands mentioned by the author Sgroi (1982).

Fourth Session

Theme: Family roles, expectations, and boundaries.
Art Directive: Draw a picture of your family doing something together.

This directive was threatening to the group members and brought about a great deal of anxiety. One member refused to draw, and two women created pictures of their family together even though both had children in extended foster placement. One individual included herself, her husband, and two younger children, while excluding all of the older children who still lived at home. Another woman portrayed the entire family, even though the perpetrator was outside the home. The remaining five members drew only the family members who lived with them, excluding the children who lived outside the home.

Harriet's picture shows herself and her daughters playing volleyball together, with the mother on one side and the children on the other, even though both her girls were in long-term foster placement. Nevertheless, the overall feeling of the artwork is one of mutual enjoyment. A net that separates the mother from her two girls is analogous to the children's current separation from her.

Karen displayed some of the family members on a camping trip. On the bottom left side of the page is her husband fishing; on the top left is herself reading a book; in the center her six-year-old son is hiking; and at the bottom righthand side her teenage daughter, the victim, is sunning herself on a rock. Karen did not draw her three older children, ages 24, 22, and 20, who lived with her, one of whom was accused of molesting his teenage sister. Karen's depiction reveals those family members with whom she is spending the most time and emotional energy. The placement of the figures is detached, and the lack of mutual activity is symbolic of the lack of family interaction (Figure 5.11).

Marie's artwork demonstrates the family's recent trip to Disneyland and included her husband, even though he was living out of the home. The image conveys a sense of happiness that Marie felt about her husband's increased visitations. Unlike the "animal family picture" of Figure 5.10, she drew herself and her husband standing together, as he participated in the care of their youngest child. As in her previous drawing, Marie again set her daughter, the victim, furthest away from her husband with herself between them. This is a

Figure 5.11.   Poor family interaction

positive indicator of Marie's new awareness of her role as her daughter's protector. During the discussion, she talked about a family trip that her victimized daughter did not participate in. She proudly told the group how her husband had comforted his crying child. He patiently explained that the reason she could not come along was because *he* had done "something very stupid" and it was all *his fault*. This statement shows that he was beginning to assume responsibility for the molestation and was trying to relieve the child of guilt.

Vicki's artwork included all of the people who currently lived in her house, watching television. She drew her son-in-law, daughter, and grandson on a sofa on the lefthand side of the page, with herself and her younger two daughters on a separate sofa to the right. When Vicki shared her picture, the therapist interpreted that the placement of the people in the drawing demonstrated an appropriate division between the two families, which could be difficult when they all lived under the same roof. Also, the placement of herself in the middle between the two sofas was evidence of her role in creating family boundaries. Vicki was pleased with the therapist's observations and talked at length about how she tried "not to interfere" in her daughter's family. She explained that she had set up a schedule for household chores so she was "not left taking care of everyone."

Vicki's picture prompted other group members to discuss how household chores were carried out in their families, an important issue for incestuous families who tend to lack clear boundaries and appropriate roles.

Fifth Session

Theme: Exploring past history and its relationship to the present.
Art Directives: (1) Draw a lifeline starting from the beginning of your life until now; (2) Mark off significant life events on the line; (3) Use different colors to represent your feelings about the events that occurred during that time.

The author explained the purpose of the directives and illustrated an example in response to the many questions group members had about the project. The mood in the room was somber. Unlike their usual interaction, the members did not talk to each other as they created their art.

Dina was the first person to share her work. Her lifeline was clearly coded and self-disclosing. Dina's childhood was marked with a dot that represented her own molestation. She was the only person who delineated and discussed such an abusive event, even though others in the group were also sexually abused as children. Further down on her lifeline she indicated her daughter's first molestation, at the age of five, by her second husband. Dina coded the later years by symbolizing the following: (1) attempts to prevent the sexual abuse from recurring; (2) attempts to get the family professional help for the molestation and for her husband's alcoholism; (3) her daughter's placement in a foster home after the incest was again disclosed; and (4) the family's battles with the court system.

Last, she drew an arch of lines over a black dot. She described this part saying that after receiving professional help for a number of years, she now felt good on the outside but was confused with a core of anger on the inside. Dina's "lifeline" conveys a conviction to work on resolving life struggles. It also exhibits the knowledge of her rage, which she hoped to dissolve in the future.

In contrast to Dina's, Karen's artwork was confusing and difficult to read. It lacked clarity in the delineation of events and the description of feelings. Although she did not participate with other group members when Dina discussed her childhood, Karen did admit she, too, felt unloved as a child. She confessed having great difficulty in telling her children that she loved them and believed it would have an adverse effect on them. Karen's discussion of this issue conveyed an apology to her daughter Marie, even though she used another daughter as an example. Marie did not respond and remained silent after her mother's painful disclosure. It was Dina who gently confronted Karen, stating that it was never too late to learn how to tell someone you love them.

Marie shared her lifeline only briefly with the group, then surprised everyone by saying she did not want to talk about it. The group knew that Marie had been molested during childhood by a family friend. Perhaps her mother Karen's presence prevented her from discussing the art. This remained an unresolved issue between mother and daughter.

One of the most dramatic and colorful lifelines was displayed by a new group member, Gina. She described her childhood as "mostly happy" until the death of her father, which occurred when she was a teenager. An upturned line in Gina's early adulthood was marked by the birth of her first daughter, the victim, and was labeled "growing up." Further down in her lifeline Gina marked another upward stroke on her graph, indicating: (1) the relationship with her current boyfriend, the perpetrator; (2) the birth of her second child; and (3) a productive work life. A downward trend stood for a period when Gina lost her job and was having troubles with her boyfriend. This was followed by a time of improvement, then a dramatic downward line symbolizing Gina's present life (Figure 5.12). Gina cried as she shared her "now" feelings of anger, confusion, and hopelessness. She was ambivalent about her daughter's molestation and stated that she felt stuck between the two people whom she loved. The expression of being stuck in the middle was articulated at various times by most of the group members. This commonality served as a support system for Gina. Several women urged her to aid her daughter and made suggestions on how she might handle her boyfriend. Other members demonstrated their concern by passing her the Kleenex box and assuring her that, "It's okay to cry."

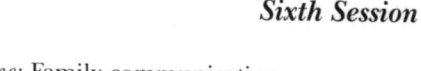
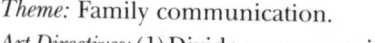

Figure 5.12. Gina asks for help

Sixth Session

Theme: Family communication.

Art Directives: (1) Divide your paper in half; (2) On one side of the paper select collage pictures that depict some things that you would like to tell your family; (3) On the other side, select some pictures that represent things that get in the way of saying what you want to say to your family.

These directives inspired the group to ask so many questions that the therapist had to repeat the instructions several times. At the group's request, the therapist gave some examples. The concept of what blocks family communication was the most difficult for the members to grasp and personalize.

Karen produced one of the more poignant pictures. On the left side of the collage were two photos of women, selected to represent the loneliness she experienced. She shared the wish that she could tell these feelings to her family. On the right side, three cheerful photos of people were chosen to illustrate the family being "too busy" with their own activities to include her (Figure 5.13, pp. 132–133). Later on when another member shared a collage, showing how caring for her elderly father got in the way of spending more time with her family, the therapist prompted Karen to talk about her own similar situation when she had to care for her mother. When Karen spoke, she presented herself as someone who always attended to the needs of other family members, yet rarely asserted her own desires. This is a common issue shared by the mothers of children who have been sexually abused.

Dina's art displayed her wish for improved family communication, relating a tendency to hide her emotions and needs from others (Figure 5.14, pp. 134–135). Dina also discussed her lack of assertiveness with her husband and her belief that this lowered her daughter's trust and regard for her.

Rene's picture depicted the first part of the directive, *"Things that you would like to tell your family."* However, she did not address the instruction to portray *"things that get in the way of saying what you want to say."* Instead, she selected two photos: (1) a family having dinner together, which represented her desire for her family to be together again; and (2) a woman taking a bubble bath, which demonstrated her wish to have more time to herself. In the second half of her collage, Rene wrote a description of her husband's part in preventing the attainment of these goals without considering her own role in these matters. When the therapist questioned her about this, it became clear that Rene, like Karen, was unassertive about getting her own needs met. She also avoided recognizing and owning her responsibility in various situations.

In this session, none of the group members pictorialized anger toward the perpetrator or directed any messages to their family of origin, even though the directive was suited to eliciting this type of information. At this initial stage of the group life, and with so many group members attempting to reconcile with the perpetrators, the direct expression of angry emotions was too threatening and, therefore, infrequently faced or disclosed.

Seventh Session

Theme: Feelings about the judicial and social service systems.
Art Directives: (1) Divide your paper in half; (2) On one side, select some pictures from the collage box that represent what it is like to have a Department of Children's Services worker assigned to you; (3) On the other side select some pictures that represent what it was like when you went to court.

The group members responded enthusiastically to the directives and were pleased to have an opportunity to discuss the emotions that were aroused by these two systems.

On the left side of Karen's collage is a picture of a woman who represents her belief that a positive caring relationship exists with herself and the social worker. On the top right side is a photo of a big man leaning over a small man, referring to a negative court experience. Next to the latter picture she wrote, "you

Figure 5.13.   A mother wishes to communicate her wishes

I AM MORE
Important than
the T.V.

I WANt my daughter
to REAlly form
A Bond of trust
with me.

Figure 5.14.   A wish for better family communication

My Emotions get in the way.

fell [sic] immtimiadated [sic] in court." Most of the group members identified with this image and responded by laughing or by commenting that they, too, felt the same way. In addition, two photos of people represent Karen's family preparing for court. A cartoon on the bottom right pictorializes Karen lying awake at night, "worrying about going to court."

Rene produced a composition that displayed her negative experiences with both her social worker and the court system. On the left side, Rene chose an image of a suit of armor to show her belief that her social worker "did not listen" to her concerns about the placement of her two sons. This photo of armor suggests that Rene needed to defend herself against the indifference of the social worker. On the right side are two photos. One is of a group of people which illustrates Rene being "nervous" and "upset" about court proceedings. The other picture is a man with a suitcase, which shows her perception that going to court was a "crazy" experience (Figure 5.15). Rene accepted the therapist's interpretation regarding the cartoon of the figure with the suitcase as representing Rene's wish to "get away from" the courtroom situation.

An evocative collage was produced by Reina, a new group member. On the top left side of the page are three images: (1) a person standing above another; (2) a woman with sunglasses; and (3) a woman with a sad expression. These magazine photographs portray her belief that at first the social worker looked down on her and was critical because her daughter had been sexually abused.

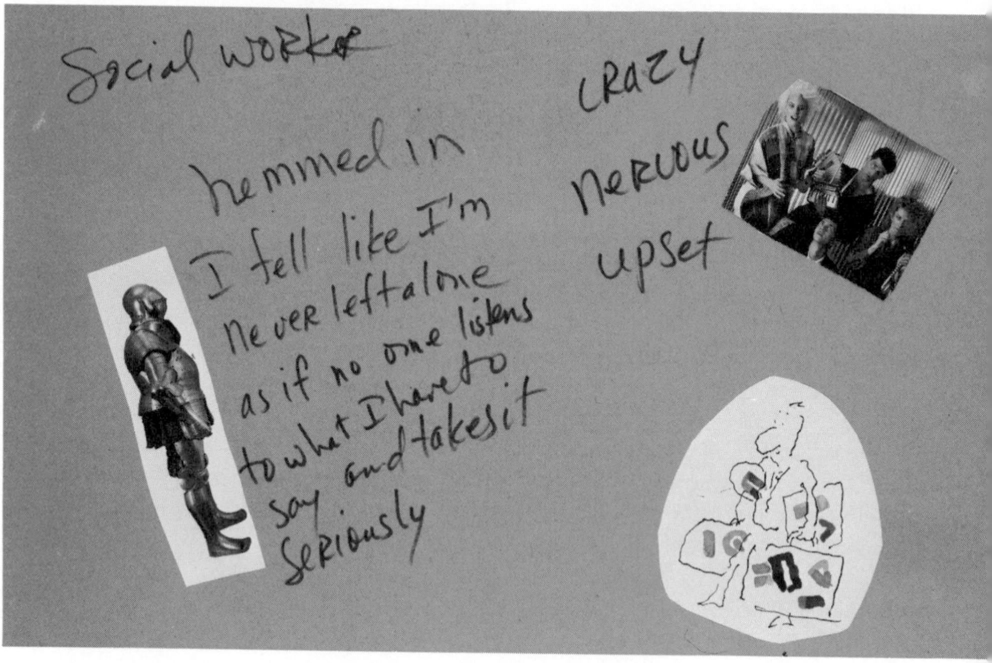

Figure 5.15.   Negative experiences with the court and social service systems

Two photos, one of a woman massaging her temples and the other of a man with a dog, demonstrates two experiences: (1) the headache that she got after the initial meeting with her social worker; and (2) the positive working relationship that she has with her social worker now. Yet, the choice of a man and dog to represent her current relationship with her social worker suggests that she still feels intimidated by her. The selection of a suit of armor on the right side of the collage pictorializes what she thought court would be like when the case came to trial. Reina thought that the courtroom experience would be a "dark, frightening one," with a little bit of "light" representing her hope that her ex-husband would get some help after being prosecuted (Figure 5.16). This member accepted and felt some relief from the therapist's interpretation that the suit of armor represented Reina, defending herself and her daughter in court.

Eighth Session

Theme: The protection of children from future sexual abuse.

Art Directive: Select some collage pictures that represent things you can do right now to protect all of your children from being molested.

The therapist anticipated that the directive would be difficult and anxiety provoking because it might evoke feelings of inadequacy about having been unable to protect their children in the past. Curiously, not one member alluded to this fact; instead, the group hesitated for only a moment before beginning the project. As members shared their art, the author was struck by the confidence shown by most group members. The message was, "As a result of what happened to me, I now know what I need to do." Only one member brought up the possibility that children could be molested again if not properly protected.

Of the seven pictures produced in this session, only three warn against "bad touches" from people who are not strangers. This seems to indicate the defense of denial among some members that intrafamilial abuse could possibly recur

One of the clearest responses to the directive was produced by Joanne. She started her picture by drawing, then continued by looking through the collage box. Shortly thereafter, Joanne stated that she could not find pictures to illustrate all of her thoughts, and augmented her art by writing a list of her ideas. Joanne wrote that she warned her children that "uncomfortable touches could come from everyone, even family members."

Reina, another group member, also produced a more complete response to the directive. On the left-hand side of the collage she pasted photos of: (1) two women dancing, which shows the importance of close family relationships; (2) a medical book, which portrays her belief in the importance of education about sexual abuse; and (3) a family sitting together, which exemplifies the central role of "open family communication." On the other side of the collage the images were of (1) a man touching a woman, which depicts Reina teaching her children

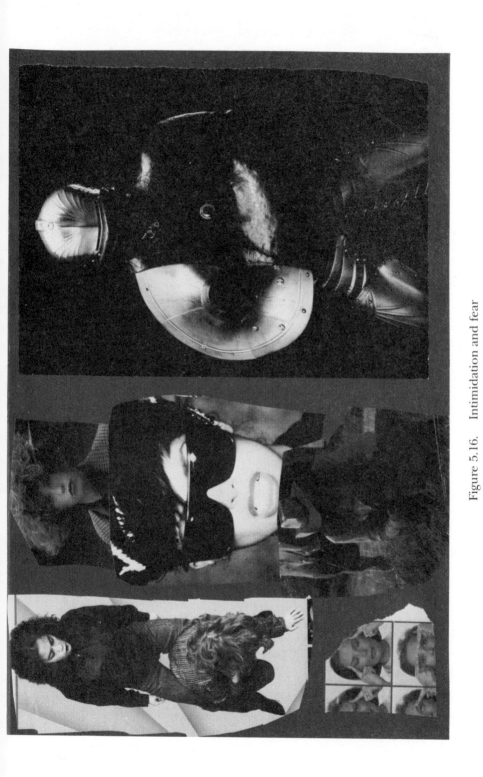

Figure 5.16.   Intimidation and fear

to recognize "bad touches"; (2) a person writing, and a picture of a woman with her hand to her ear, which indicates her role in listening to her children for signs of distress; (3) a woman on the phone, which denotes Reina getting help when it is needed; and (4) a picture of a girl with an upraised arm, which represents the importance of fostering the children's self-esteem so they will be better able to avoid "bad touches" (Figure 5.17). Reina was the only group member to consider the importance of self-esteem, as well as education, for the effective protection of her children.

Harriet's art contains images of: (1) a man in a car, (2) a man on a bike, and (3) a burglar. These display her belief in warning children against going off with strangers. She also used these photos to discuss her daughter's first molestation by a stranger. As this woman shared her art, she related an incident when her victimized daughter had recently gone to a stranger's house after school to ask to use the telephone. She added that fortunately the child was unharmed. The group responded with shock and attempted to comfort Harriet as she talked about this incident. Harriet repeated her family therapist's statement that her daughter "continued to put herself in dangerous situations."

Harriet's report helped to remind all of the participants about the necessity of consistently educating and protecting their children. This is essential, since those who had already been abused are at the greatest risk of being molested again.

Marie's collage is an effort to strengthen herself as parent and protector in her family. On the left side she picked photos of children who represented her own children. On the right side, she pasted two photos of an eagle and one of a woman, which describes her belief that it was her role to watch for signs of distress in her children and to assure them that they could get help from her. Marie did not include any reference to educating her children about sexual abuse. This omission is significant and exhibits her insecurity about taking on this role at the present time.

Dina took a social, rather than personal view about the problem of preventing children from being sexually abused. Her collage included: (1) a photo of three old women with disapproving facial expressions, which pictorialized her belief in educating teachers, ministers, police, and parents about sexual abuse; (2) a photo of a family with two children, which represented the importance of encouraging open communication and education in the family; and (3) a photo of a chorus line bowing, which expressed the importance of maintaining support groups.

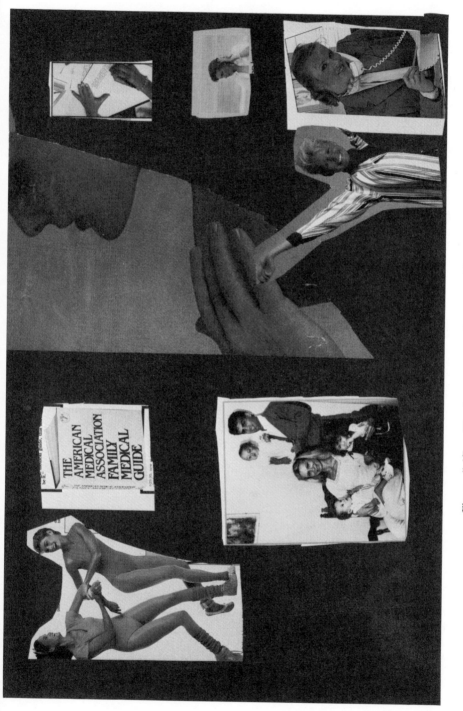

Figure 5.17. The importance of strong self-esteem

CONCLUDING REMARKS

The final directive used with this group of mothers of incestuously abused children was designed to explore group members' perceptions of their art therapy experience. In addition to the inherent therapeutic value of this directive, it was also useful in establishing an optimum treatment plan for this population.

The majority of the group members reported an initial hesitancy in regard to art therapy, followed by feelings of acceptance, then enjoyment. One member verbalized liking art therapy, although her art depictions alluded to the experience as "child's play." Another group member reported negative feelings about a previous art therapy experience; however, she related having very positive feelings about this group. Two other individuals addressed the issues that brought them into the group, rather than directly addressing their feelings about the modality. It is this therapist's belief that the group members' avoidance of giving any negative feedback was directly related to their treatment issues of passivity, poor self-esteem, lack of assertiveness, and lack of trust in mental health institutions.

A consensus was expressed by the group that the art helped them to focus on specific issues. With this population, one of the most important functions of the art task is that it provides a way for less verbally assertive members to participate. The ability of the imagery to communicate information was seen in the artwork of the group members, many of whom rarely talked when not sharing their pictures. Several of the participants expressed their appreciation that they were not required to discuss their imagery, and that the therapist did not probe further for unconscious material. A nonconfrontive style is critically important with this population due to their trust issues and their fears of feeling exposed. Group members expressed a preference for collage media over drawing, and a greater degree of comfort was noted in depicting incest and family issues through this media and in using these pictures as a bridge to group discussion.

In general, the necessity of maintaining an open group not only affected group process and development, but the usefulness of some of the directives as well. Although each of the directives had therapeutic value, group resistance (particularly from new members) was increased when the themes did not directly relate to immediate, crisis issues. A closed group would provide optimum conditions for greater exploration of incest dynamics, psychodynamic issues, and group interactive issues.

REFERENCES

Carozza, P. M., & Heirsteiner, C. (1982). Young female incest victims in treatment: Stages of growth seen with a group art therapy model. *Clinical Social Work Journal, 10*(3), 165–175.

Dietz, C. A., & Craft, J. L. (1980). Family dynamics of incest: A new perspective. *Social Casework: The Journal of Contemporary Social Work, 69,* 602–609.

Feldman, L. (1984). Incest research: Young victims drawings may give clues to crime. *The Emmisary,* February, *16*(2), 3–6.

Finkelhor, D. (1980). Risk factors in the sexual victimization of children. *Child Abuse and Neglect, 4,* 265–273.

Goodwin, J. M., McCarty, T., & DiVasto, P. (1981). Prior incest in mothers of abused children. *Child Abuse and Neglect, 5,* 87–95.

Gordy, P. L. (1983). Group work that supports adult victims of childhood incest. *Social Casework: The Journal of Contemporary Social Work, 64*(5), 300–307.

Herman, J. (1983). Recognition and treatment of incestuous families. *International Journal of Family Therapy, 5*(2), 81–99.

Hillman, D., & Solek-Tefft, J. (1988). *Spiders and Flies: Help for Parents and Teachers of Sexually Abused Children.* Lexington, MA: Lexington Books.

Howard, M., & Jakab, I. (1968). Case studies of molested children and their art productions. *Psychiatry and Art, 2,* 72–89.

Justice, B., & Justice, R. (1979). *The Broken Taboo: Sex in the Family.* New York: Human Sciences Press.

Lustig, N., Dresser, J. W., Spellman, S. W., & Murry, T. B. (1966). Incest: A family group survival pattern. *Archives of General Psychiatry, 14,* 31–40.

McIntyre, K. (1981). Role of mothers in father-daughter incest: A feminist analysis. *Social Work, 26,* 462–466.

Niatove, C. (1982). Art therapy with sexually abused children. In S. Sgroi (Ed.), *Handbook of Clinical Intervention in Child Sexual Abuse* (pp. 269–308). Lexington, MA: Lexington Books.

Press, A., Morris, H., & Sandza, R. (1981). An epidemic of incest. *Newsweek,* November 30, p. 68.

Prince, J. (1981). Father-daughter incest: An attempt to maintain the family and meet human needs? *Family and Community Health, 4,* 35–44.

Russell, D. (1983). The incidence and prevalence of intra-familial and extra-familial sexual abuse of female children. *Child Abuse and Neglect, 7,* 133–146.

Selby, J. W., Calhoun, L. G., Jones, J. M., & Matthews, L. (1980). Families of incest: A collation of clinical impressions. *International Journal of Social Psychiatry, 26,* 7–16.

Sgroi, S. (Ed.) (1982). *Handbook of Clinical Intervention in Child Sexual Abuse.* Lexington, MA: Lexington Books.

Sgroi, S. (Ed.) (1988). *Vulnerable Populations, Vol. 1.* Lexington, MA: Lexington Books.

Summit, R. (1983). Recognition and treatment of child sexual abuse. *Coping with Pediatric Illness* (pp. 115–172). New York: Spectrum Publications.

Taubman, S. (1984). Incest in context. *Social Work, 29*(1), 35–40.

Will, D. (1983). Approaching the incestuous and sexually abusive family. *Journal of Adolescence, 6,* 229–246.

Yalom, I. D. (1975). *The Theory and Practice of Group Psychotherapy.* New York: Basic Books.

Zuelzer, M. B., & Reposa, R. E. (1983). Mothers in incestuous families. *International Journal of Family Therapy, 5*(2), 98–110.

Chapter 6

Art Therapy with AIDS Patients

Ann Bussard and Susan Kleinman

AIDS is often called a modern-day plague. Those who have contracted the disease are viewed by some as today's lepers. The word "aids" used to mean tools or objects that help people complete a task, create a design, or assist another human being. Now the term "AIDS," which stands for Acquired Immune Deficiency Syndrome, is equated with incredible physical, mental, and emotional losses, stigma, and ultimately . . . death.

The Centers for Disease Control in Atlanta reports there have been over 124,980 persons diagnosed with AIDS and 76,000 AIDS-related deaths since the first deaths before 1981 up through February, 1990 (Centers for Disease Control, 1990). Because the fatality rate is staggering, living with AIDS can be described as a living death.

This chapter begins with an overview of the psychological needs of patients with AIDS, followed by a discussion of how support groups and individual treatment can be effective. The chapter concludes with a description of how the issues that AIDS patients must confront can be seen in their artwork and how the art process can provide relief and support both to groups and to individuals.

AIDS produces prolonged periods of physical and psychological suffering. It remains a socially stigmatizing disease, associated in the public consciousness with socially stigmatized groups (Namir, 1985).

The diagnosis of AIDS creates a variety of responses in the patient, ranging from shock and denial, to anxiety, anger, and depression. Patients also experience fear, dread, suicidal impulses, guilt, sadness, helplessness, betrayal, regret, social withdrawal, and isolation.

People with terminal illnesses such as AIDS usually experience intense emotional states. Because their lives are devoid of customary diversions, distractions, and daily habits, they may feel anxious and attempt to bind this anxiety by developing obsessive cognitive styles and ruminative thinking. These patients vacillate between anger, guilt, rage, depression, fear, and sadness. Their emotions can fluctuate within the course of a day, creating an exhausting roller coaster effect. Mercurial swings between hope and helplessness are sometimes due to alterations in their medical condition, doctor's reports, and frequent news items about their disease.

Many people with AIDS have an intense need for mental health support because of these psychological issues and the accompanying fears and stigma. Research has demonstrated that psychological factors may increase a patient's susceptibility to disease, influence the course of the disease, or contribute to both health-promoting and health-risking behaviors.

Moynihan, Christ, and Silver (1988) describe the complicated issues of AIDS patients, some of whom live many months or years with chronic illness, while others die only a few months after diagnosis. They identify four social and psychological tasks each individual is confronted with after diagnosis: (1) maintenance of a meaningful quality of life in the face of disease and the threat of death; (2) toleration of disfigurement and loss of function; (3) confrontation of existential and spiritual questions; and (4) preparation of surviving friends and family.

Individual therapy and support groups have been essential components of treatment for the AIDS patient. Both tend to combine theories from separate clinical fields: psychotherapy, self-help, and community support systems. Franzino, Geren, and Meiman (1976) emphasize that group leaders should take on a nondirective, nonconfrontational, supportive stance, taking care not to challenge the defense mechanisms that AIDS patients need in order to cope with the pain of their terminal illness. This treatment approach is similarly appropriate when working with an individual.

GROUP ART THERAPY

Short-term art therapy groups provide support to AIDS patients and help them cope with the psychological and emotional issues related to their disease. Because these patients must also face physical pain and discomfort, appropriate and flexible treatment goals are critical. Art tasks are specifically designed to integrate the problems and concerns that AIDS patients must grapple with. Day-to-day coping issues and problem solving are dealt with through imagery, metaphor, and verbalization.

The groups described in this chapter contracted to meet once a week for six to eight consecutive weeks. A verbal commitment provided the group members with a time-limited experience. The group became a source of immediate support and acceptance, against the unbearable uncertainty and vulnerability the disease process generates. Variability in attendance is to be expected, due to lack of transportation, doctor's appointments, or the progression of the illness.

Session length for group sharing can vary from about 45 to 90 minutes, depending on the number of participants and their physical stamina. Because of the intimate and powerful content of each meeting, groups are ideally limited to four to six persons. The authors' experiences were with groups of men between the ages of 21 and 41. The insights, goals, and directives discussed in this chapter reflect this age range.

A variety of media can be offered. General precautions should be kept in mind about bodily secretions, such as those from open sores, coming in contact with the supplies which then are communally used. Medical resources at two hospitals advised the authors, however, that shared art supplies, with prudent hygienic attention to usage, do not pose a known threat to the health of group members.

The overall aim of the art therapy group is to provide support and a forum for ventilation, problem solving, and mutual understanding. Members are encouraged to find ways to cope with the myriad of feelings and issues so painfully associated with the AIDS disease. Through the art process, group members can be nurtured by the colorful media and the creative opportunity for self-expression. The resultant imagery evokes group support and serves as a source of ventilation for the sometimes overwhelming emotions. Consequently, participants often openly acknowledge the support and feedback received during group sessions.

The following sections focus attention on how the art process helps participants move from isolation and loneliness to connection and empowerment, from denial to acceptance, from loss of control and anxiety to relief, and from despair to hope. Anger, loss, mortality, and fear also play prominent roles in group members' artwork.

Denial Unmasked: Isolation Lessened

Denial is commonly seen in persons with life-threatening diseases. It can be both a destructive and a supportive defense mechanism. As one of the most prominent reactions to the AIDS diagnosis, denial can manifest itself in acting-out behaviors. Some individuals may ignore their diagnosis and proceed to engage in unsafe sex, drug use, or other self-destructive behaviors. In a more positive context, denial can serve to minimize the patient's overwhelming fear, anger, and helplessness. Some patients with terminal illnesses who utilize denial exhibit less anxiety, more hope, and have a longer survival rate. With hope and purposeful ignorance as an outgrowth of denial, individuals who have contracted this illness may be able to continue to experience life as meaningful and perhaps extendible.

Conversely, there is a price to pay for refusing to acknowledge reality. Denial as a defense against the psychological pain of the disease can close off avenues to shared time with others. A complicated distance between patients and their relatives or friends can be created by the "lie" or secret everyone keeps to avoid confronting the poor prognosis.

Choosing to attend an art therapy group is a first step in decreasing denial and the resultant isolation. As with any group, an initial goal is to help facilitate cohesion among the members by creating a forum for safe self-expression. Group connection is especially important with members who have AIDS, since many of them experience isolation from employment, friends, or family. With the AIDS diagnosis, patients often give up or lose their usual social diversions— spending a great deal of time alone.

Barry, a frail-looking, 33-year-old artist, had been diagnosed with AIDS one year prior to participation in an art therapy group. He was involved in a long-term monogamous relationship for the previous five years. His lover had been supportive, both emotionally and financially. Barry, who had previously been employed as a photographer, became too ill to work. He found it difficult to rely on his lover for money, since he had always taken pride in being independent. Although this patient was involved in a verbal support group, he was especially interested in participating in an art group because of his creative background.

Initially, as an artist, Barry intuitively interpreted the unconscious imagery of his fellow group members. Yet when the group interpreted his imagery, he denied its underlying meaning.

Barry was given an initial directive to *choose four to six collage pictures to introduce yourself on a personal level; after the pictures are pasted down, write something about what the images mean, revealing as little or as much as you wish.* Barry became absorbed in the selection of photo collage pictures, as well as in the overall composition of his artwork. He took a long time to abstract portions of the pictures, turning several images sideways to form a design. By utilizing compulsivity as a defense, he filled in the space surrounding the picture of the orange, as if to support it, with a heavy application of blue oil pastel. It was necessary to ask him to stop in order for the group's discussion to begin.

Images of a solitary deer drinking water from a smooth lake, a lace collar cut away from a portrait of an Elizabethan queen, an orange, a furry puppy, and the reflection of a very shiny floor, placed upside down were chosen (Figure 6.1). When it was Barry's turn to share his art, he chose to focus on an artistic viewpoint of the textures he used, rather than to deal with personal material.

This man, who had helped the other group members see the feelings contained in their artwork, was only able to explain his own choices in design terms. When the group pointed out that the *deer* looked vulnerable, Barry stopped to consider the meaning behind the photograph. A discussion was triggered when one of the two group leaders mentioned that the orange was "a

Figure 6.1.   Textures reveal vulnerability

food item." Participants described their "lack of taste" due to medications. Barry then volunteered that the world of a person with AIDS is often without texture because of the many losses, including physical capacities and food tastes. The therapist reflected back to Barry that his choice of a texture theme poignantly revealed his concerns about these losses.

Several days later, during a phone conversation with this same clinician, Barry said he had been thinking about his collage and realized the orange, in "the position of a head," represented how all the medications he had to take made him feel inhuman, like a vegetable.

Ultimately, this artwork helped Barry express and explore his feelings of vulnerability and share a side effect of the disease which everyone could relate to. As the group progressed, Barry said he preferred group art therapy because through this modality "people got close faster and talked about more important issues."

Anger Voiced and Contained Through Art Process

Anger is probably the most powerful and—when internalized or misdirected—the most destructive of the emotions felt by persons with AIDS. Through the use of imagery, this dominant feeling can be openly expressed and visibly contained by the media. Symbolically, the modality allows free expression, while offering safe boundaries through the size of the paper, the amount of time allowed for completion of the artwork, and appropriate clinical interventions.

During one art therapy session, the group members were instructed to (1) *think about the things that have made you angry since you were diagnosed with AIDS;* and (2) *draw symbols or choose collage pictures to express those feelings.*

Ronald, a 21-year-old Black man, had been diagnosed two months before the group's formation. He used denial as a defense to a far greater extent than other members, because only recently he had discovered he was seriously ill. Ronald lived with a male roommate, who had tested positive for the AIDS virus. This individual was asymptomatic and not practicing safe sex. Ronald projected most of his anger about the disease onto his roommate, believing him to be the source of the disease. His mother was one of his caretakers. She was an extremely strong and protective woman who made many decisions for her son.

While Ronald was drawing a dollar bill, he laughed aloud (Figure 6.2). His line quality was shaky and jagged, showing either his anxiety or the effects of the medications he was taking. The money was missing a face, suggesting emptiness and the currency's worthlessness.

When his turn came to speak about his artwork, Ronald claimed he was not angry at anything. As the artwork was explored, Ronald became aware of his rage about the high cost of medical care and medications. He continued by saying his picture also reminded him of a fight he had with his mother who was

Figure 6.2. The worthless dollar

staying at his house to care for him. This young man described an incident with her, where he regressed to the point of throwing food. It became evident that anger was the result of Ronald's struggles with reconciliation of dependency issues, typical of the conflict the terminally ill person experiences. The financial strain depicted by Ronald's drawing symbolized his loss of control and thereby his self-sufficiency.

Philip was diagnosed with AIDS less than a year prior to attending an art therapy group. His body was attacked by the opportunistic infections of Kaposi's sarcoma and toxoplasmosis. The toxoplasmosis had damaged his central nervous system, causing a stroke and leaving him with arm and hand tremors. A 37-year-old social worker, he was fired from his job because of AIDS. Philip's family had been very supportive when they learned of his diagnosis. His mother came to care for him and other family members had flown in for visits. Philip was living alone and had not been involved in a relationship for a number of years.

During the same session described above, Philip used collage to voice his anger. One picture portrayed a drawing of a man printed in a computerlike fashion (Figure 6.3). Philip said this image represented his rage over the large number of tests he had been subjected to, which made him feel depersonalized. Another photo of an older couple enjoying each other's company depicted the "anger" he felt about the disruption he had caused his parents. Philip's mother had moved away from her home and family to look after him. The graveyard image, with the peasant woman holding flowers next to the burial place of a young girl, evoked an angry declaration, "I'm not ready to go there yet!" The representation may have unconsciously represented Philip's fear of dying young and leaving his mother to tend to his grave. The picture of an older

Figure 6.3.   Anger and depersonalization

woman with a gun in her hand symbolized his angry feelings about "the bitch who had me fired from my job."

Barry also created a collage that expressed his rage with medical issues and suffering (Figure 6.4). The medical system and its hold on Barry, were symbolized by the following pictures: (1) a masked doctor with a monkey image appearing to be artfully connected to him; (2) a crippled girl on crutches walking alone down a hallway; and (3) an elegant washbasin with hands postured to parallel its design.

At first, Barry was unable to free associate to the picture of the sink, claiming it to be an "icon." One of the authors wondered if it might represent the constant hand washing of medical staff and Barry agreed with that interpretation. Effigies of Saint Theresa and Saint Sebastian, noted for their suffering and eventual martyrdom, were also included in his art. The collage poignantly reveals the intensity of Barry's pain and his anger at his powerlessness against the dread disease of AIDS.

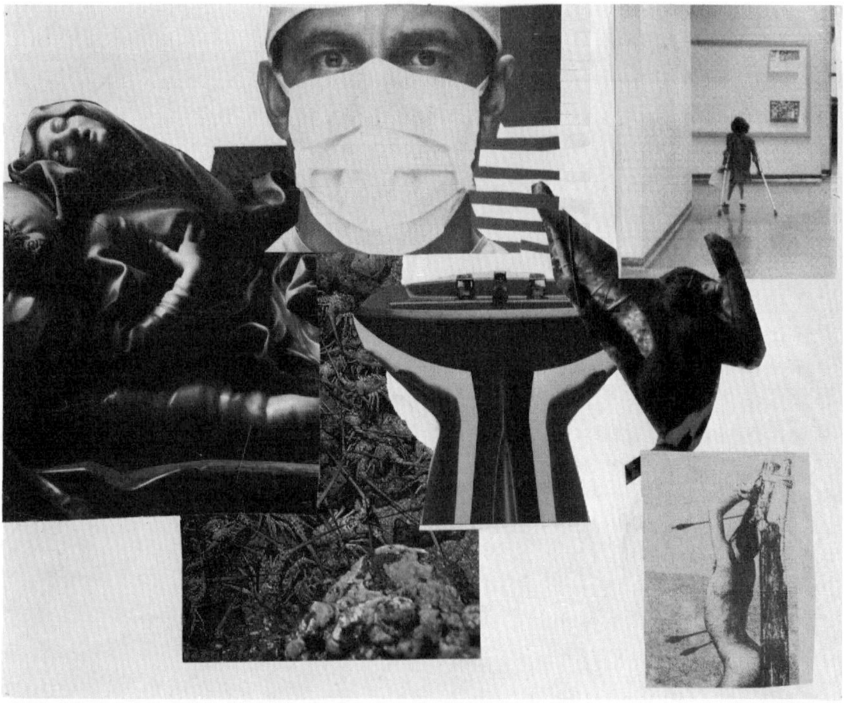

Figure 6.4.　Anger with medicine

Figure 6.5.　"Waste"

Jonathan was diagnosed with AIDS in the form of pneumocystis carinii pneumonia nearly two years prior to attending the art therapy group. He looked younger than his 32 years and maintained his attractiveness despite a considerable weight loss. Jonathan lived with a roommate and was unable to work because he tired easily. Nevertheless, he was able to care for himself and get around on his motorcycle. Jonathan had a few close friends who were generally supportive. Because of their similarities in age and lifestyle, however, they felt threatened and were reluctant to listen to his discussions on AIDS. When Jonathan was a child, his parents divorced and his grandparents became his caretakers. Recently, Jonathan's grandparents severed all contact with him after learning he was homosexual and had AIDS. Jonathan arranged to visit his grandparents to attempt a reconciliation but was traumatized when they left him stranded at the airport.

In response to the directive on anger, Jonathan chose a calendar page with days marked off and a picture of the artist Vincent Van Gogh, whose ear is bandaged (Figure 6.5). Jonathan wrote "Waste" next to the calendar. He had been having problems with his drug-using roommate that week and chose to focus his anger on his roommate, saying the week had been a "waste." The days crossed out on the calendar, the picture of the angst-ridden artist who died very young, and the word "waste" seemed to reflect the limited time left and the waste of a young life.

Symbols for Hope

When faced with a terminal illness, hope can be the AIDS patient's reason for continuing to struggle for life, to hold out for the long-awaited cure. In an art therapy group, the imagery can serve as a potent reflection of self-found hope, in spite of insurmountable odds.

Mark, a 38-year-old former retail employee, was a participant in an art therapy group held at a residential AIDS shelter. He had attempted to maintain a regular lifestyle with a special friend, but had to give up his independence and move to the shelter because of pneumocystis and shingles. He had a very close relationship with his mother, even though she found her son's lifestyle difficult to accept.

To facilitate personal control and nurturance, a directive was given to *choose three or four collage pictures to show ways you help yourself feel better.* During previous groups, Mark had trouble grasping the pens. Although a thin, weakened man, suffering from the wasting syndrome, he quietly proceeded to create a moving testimony to his positive outlook (Figure 6.6). (The writing has been darkened to make his words more apparent.)

Figure 6.6. "Happiness"

In his collage titled "Happiness," Mark used colorful images to display themes of importance to him. He chose two pictures dealing with the meaning of friendship: one, of three people sledding, called "having fun with friends," and another of a man and a woman enjoying and sharing a soda, named "good times." The theme of "father/son relationships" emerges in the form of two pictures of fathers playing with their sons. Of particular interest is the picture of two soldiers in a moving embrace, titled "showing emotions." Perhaps due to his weakened state, his own isolation, or his acceptance of his fate, Mark had resisted talking about any negative feelings. The choice of the two soldiers, who are able to express emotional intensity, seems to be a metaphor for Mark's own war with the disease and his growing willingness to share his own feelings with his peers.

Individuality Supported

One of the losses often experienced by AIDS victims is the loss of individual identity. These patients are living statistics whose self-image gradually decays under the onslaught of personal losses. It is important to use group support as a means of fostering self-esteem and personality traits.

In another session Mark participated in, a wide choice of media was offered to stimulate creativity and self-expression. To help the men identify a sense of self, they were directed to *trace or draw your hand(s), then decorate it to symbolize yourself.*

Slowly and weakly Mark combined collage images with a lightly drawn tracing of his left hand (Figure 6.7). (The tracing has been darkened to make the hand more apparent.) The five pictures correspond to what he wrote on each of the five fingers. Counterclockwise, from bottom left, "Style-class" referred to the vertically positioned picture of the torso of a black man in a white suit. Mark included a picture of a man who appears to be yelling as he is standing in an automobile with his upper body revealed through the sun roof. Mark titled this picture "Having a good time." The third photo, a profile of a young woman, is captioned, "Beauty." The large pocket watch, which seems to dominate the collage, is titled, "Pensive thoughts." The fifth photo, a glass being filled with orange juice, is named, "A good drink." Mark said these five areas represented his interests in life, although many of them were lost due to the illness. The issue of time was explored through the watch image. Mark only focused on the appreciation of its beauty and ignored any connection with his terminal disease.

Overall, the artwork helped the patients in this group express their individuality creatively. This task facilitated understanding among the participants and helped them "see" themselves, and each other, as viable human beings, not just sick and dying people.

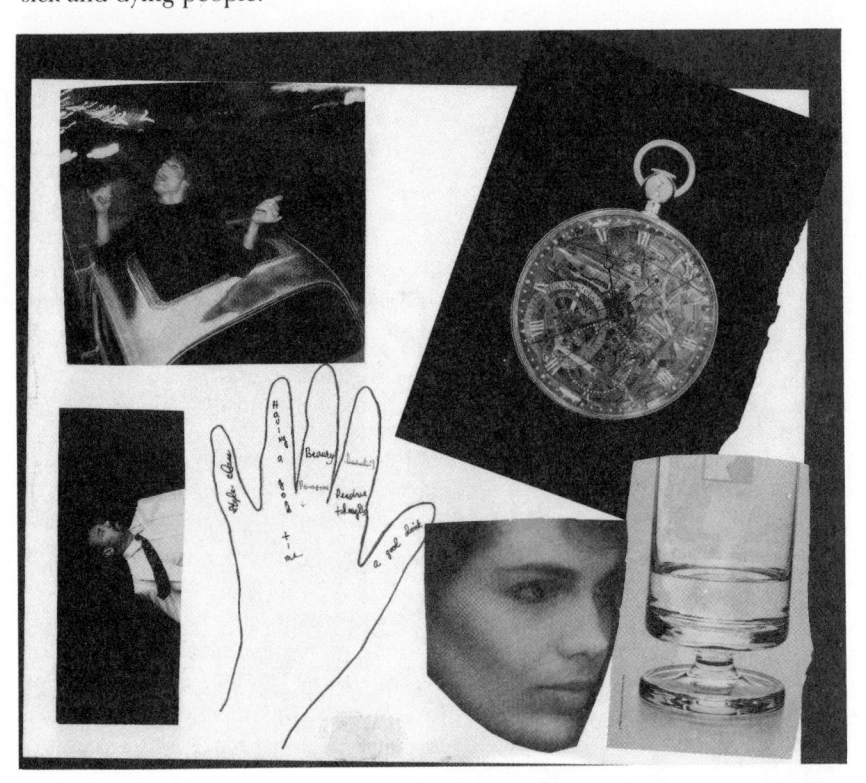

Figure 6.7. The pocket watch

An Exploration of Loss

An art therapy group can utilize the *metaphor* to address the many losses that accompany AIDS and to find a means of coping with them. The following illustrates how this issue was brought to the fore with two men with AIDS. Participants in this group included Ross and William.

Ross, an anxious, 39-year-old Black man, was suffering from bleeding ulcers in addition to his AIDS diagnosis. This man was reared in a sexually abusive family by a domineering and possessive mother. Ross had previously worked in maintenance and housekeeping. As his illnesses progressed, Ross lost his job and moved to the AIDS residence.

William was a 41-year-old oncology nurse, with a friendly and outgoing nature that seemed to defy his terminal prognosis. A resident at the AIDS shelter, he too had struggled with his family's disapproval of his bisexual lifestyle. He had, however, recently received support from his family while battling Kaposi's sarcoma. During one session, William notified the group he would be leaving the house. Because he was feeling better, William wanted to return to his own apartment, go back to work part-time, and restore some of his original independence.

To help the group address the issue of William's departure, the men were directed to *draw about saying good-bye.*

Although anxious and ready to leave the group early, Ross completed a three-picture collage which visually portrays his sad feelings about William's impending departure (Figure 6.8). For the first photo, Ross wrote "am getting sad" underneath the picture of a dejected-looking woman whose reflection is mirrored in the chrome of a toaster that has burning toast popping out of it. In the second picture, a whale appears to be licking the side of a smiling woman's face. This photo appears to be both pleasant and threatening. The large whale, although probably trained, could easily overwhelm and harm this woman. Titled "It [sic] was glad to have him here. I hope he don't go," this image seemed to reflect Ross's ambivalent—perhaps angry—feelings about the loss of his friend. The third picture is of a man, holding onto the outside of a helicopter, pointing and looking down, next to a passenger who is sitting securely inside the helicopter. Ross wrote, "He's leaving us now." The potential danger the photo depicts suggested Ross's unconscious fears about William's movement away from the safety of the residence.

Prior to making the "goodbye picture," William completed a drawing about how he was feeling that day. The previous weekend had been a difficult one for him, with feelings of depression weighing him down. William said the drawing showed how he was moving through the depression into a better place (Figure 6.9). William explained that the stick figure was walking through rain and a gray

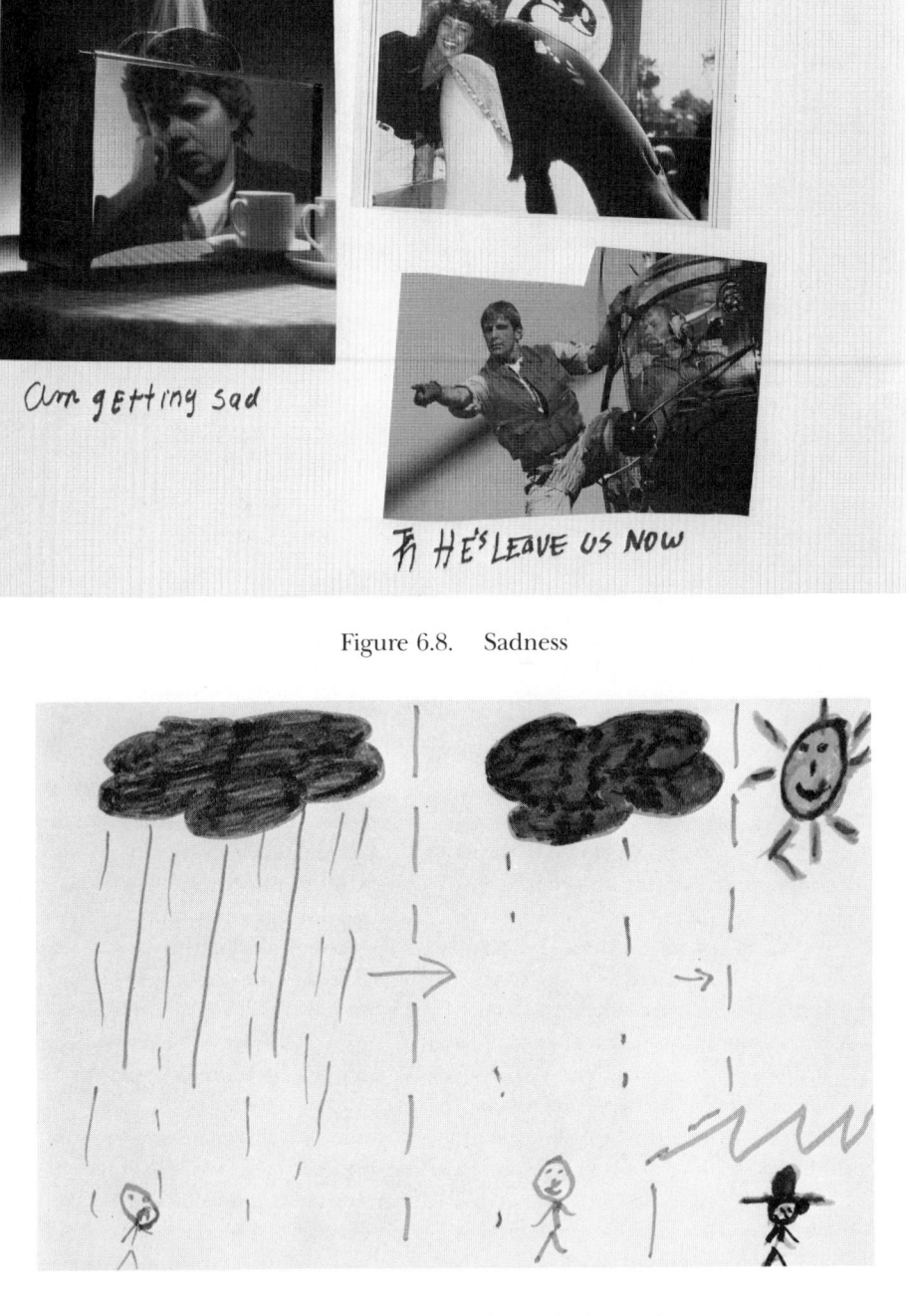

Figure 6.8.　Sadness

Figure 6.9.　Movement through depression

From Hea

Figure 6.10.　"From health to the desert"

cloud. These symbols represented his depression. In the next stage, the rain seems to be sprinkling only and the cloud is colored with purple and blue, not gray. The purple cloud may have been a metaphor for the purple Kaposi's sarcoma lesions covering William's eyelids, causing him to look like he had two swollen black eyes. The third section of the drawing depicts the figure, now red-colored, moving into a space with a smiling yellow sun. William's addition of a jagged line above the stick man, however, serves to isolate the figure, which appears burdened with a large hat and looks smaller and more vulnerable than before.

William's second piece of artwork, again, seems to reflect movement and appears to be a goodbye to himself, that is, the person he once was (Figure 6.10, pp. 158–159). In his collage titled "From Health to the Desert," William surrounds a picture of a camel caravan crossing a barren desert with images reflecting the positive aspects of his past: relationships, grocery shopping and enjoying food, and bathing a dog. Included is a photo of a nurse giving a man a shot. While this picture reminded William of his profession as a nurse, it also reflected the role change from caregiver to care receiver. Although William was preparing to return to what he hoped would be an autonomous life outside the residence, the artwork revealed the opposite. He exhibited the losses he had encountered. Even the title, "From Health to the Desert," predicted his eventual return and death in the AIDS shelter.

When working with those who are terminally ill, it is advisable to contrast an exploration of loss with specific sources of hope. This two-pronged approach allows the participants an opportunity both to ventilate their negative emotions and to activate coping mechanisms to encourage a sense of control and to increase self-esteem.

In a group Barry participated in, the therapists first passed out precut, oblong pieces of paper, each drawn with lines dividing the ovals into thirds. The members were directed to *draw, write, or use collage to express the many kinds of losses, unexpected gains, and strengths you have experienced since your diagnosis.* The goal of this directive was to help the group deal with the issue of loss in a manner that would provide structure and contain overwhelming feelings. The three equal sections gave the members uniform opportunity to address the negative aspects as well as the positive ones.

Barry, the frail artist, chose to combine drawing with collage (Figure 6.11). To illustrate loss, he placed a picture of gowned and gloved medical technicians working in a sterile environment in the left wedge. He talked about how he had tentatively chosen this collage picture during the very first session (the one when he talked about textures), but, unable to deal with the imagery at that time, he had put the photo aside. Connected to the collage picture is a drawing of a slablike rectangular form which could be viewed as a mortuary slab or tombstone. In the top section, which represented his strengths, Barry placed a photo of *a bull* next to a drawing of a prickly cactus. The artist said his "bullishness" gave him the strength to survive in the harsh desert world of AIDS.

Figure 6.11.   Oblong collage: losses, unexpected gains, strengths

Unexpected gains were expressed in the bottom portion of a shark photo on the edge of a picture of *a couple trying to crawl through a maze to reach a baby.* Barry admitted that it had not been easy to work out his relationship with his parents and especially with his formerly abusive father, but gains had been made during a recent visit home.

Sexuality Explored Through the Media

Sexuality and its perceived relationship to the AIDS virus is an important topic to explore with group members. Ideally, this sensitive subject should be examined as part of the middle phase of a group, when cohesion has been established and the members can tolerate this type of investigation.

Group members were directed to (1) *use the art materials to show how your sexuality has changed since the illness,* and (2) *show how the changes have affected your self-esteem.*

The Soviets have made Cuban dictator Fidel Castro their point man in Africa.

28

Figure 6.12.   Sexual issues explored

In a survey, 94 percent of the Hispanics listed tradition, such

Philip, the social worker, made a collage whose dominant theme was loss of control (Figure 6.12, pp. 162–163). He said that if he passed the AIDS virus on to another person he "would feel like a murderer." His unhappiness with his body image was echoed by a small photo of men working out in a gym, placed top center. Philip said exercise was a former activity, now lost, due to his weakened state. He reminisced about the days before he had AIDS. Pointing to the top right picture of a wedding party, he explained that on Halloween many gay men would dress up in wedding gowns and dresses.

Philip's confusion about what to do with his sexual feelings was shown by a cartoon, positioned bottom right, of a man huddled and hiding under a desk. He admitted he was now "hiding" from those feelings. Many of Philip's collage pictures were extended beyond the edges of the background paper. The expanded boundaries seemed to reflect how overwhelming the exploration of sexual issues could be.

Another member, Ronald, selected oil pastels to symbolize his feelings through bands of color drawn vertically on the page. He pointed out that at first he used black as the color of depression and hopelessness to state how sad he was that he could never have sex again. The rainbow-type effect he created, however, gradually progressed to brighter colors, ending with yellow which symbolized hope and the wish to have a relationship once again.

The Art as a Diagnostic Tool

Current literature reveals high rates of brain compromise in patients afflicted with the AIDS virus (Buckingham & Van Gorp, 1988). Not only must patients endure physical, emotional, and psychological debilitation associated with the disease, they are also susceptible to AIDS-related dementia. The artwork can be helpful in supporting the therapist's initial diagnosis and reflecting the diminishing mental capacities of the patient.

For example, Alvin was a 33-year-old Hispanic male who had been diagnosed four months previous to joining the group. As a member of an alcoholic family, he started abusing drugs and alcohol when he was ten and was a male prostitute from that time until he was 30 years old. Three years prior to the group he was severely mugged, beaten, and stabbed, and was not expected to live. After recovering, he became active in Alcoholics Anonymous (AA) and increased his self-esteem by helping others in AA and by working as a housekeeper. He rarely saw his father or siblings. Alvin lived close to his mother, who was described as being "more like a sister." He behaved in a very flirtatious manner with the other participants. Alvin referred to himself as a "woman," revealing that he had dressed in "drag" and worn make-up. He frequently used self-depreciating humor as a defense. He said he had experienced "intimacy" only within a sexual context. Because of AIDS, Alvin became especially isolated and was struggling to find new ways to relate to others.

Alvin came to a session after having had a particularly difficult morning. He had suffered from diarrhea and vomiting and was still feeling nauseous. He had also had a fight with his mother, the primary caretaker. During group discussions, Alvin either attempted to dominate all conversations, or interrupted the group by constantly leaving the room. Although he initially said that he was very happy that day, the amount of agitation, neediness, and inability to express his needs prompted the therapists to explore the underlying reasons for his agitation. When questioned, Alvin appeared to be relieved that the therapists did not "buy" his happy act. However, this moment of understanding and sharing of real feelings was not enough to contain him and he continued his intrusive behavior. Alvin's history revealed he had previous psychological problems which were exacerbated by the AIDS diagnosis. His otherwise inexplicable demeanor suggested decompensation and early signs of AIDS-related dementia.

The group Alvin was in was directed to *draw or use collage pictures to show how you feel at this moment.* Alvin's behavior was clearly reflected in his art (Figure 6.13). His oil pastel drawing contained several tepees drawn in the top portion of the paper. Although a grounding line is present, the drawing appears to be floating on the page, mirroring Alvin's inability to remain seated and focused. In the right corner is a church with a cross on its roof. Alvin said the tepee was a "spiritual symbol" for him. In this drawing, his tepees resemble tombstones in a pastoral-looking church cemetery. Perhaps Alvin unconsciously drew a burial ground, suggesting his own conflict about death.

Figure 6.13.   Tepees

During an activity at the end of this group session, Alvin's regressive behavior was unconsciously revealed in a pass-around drawing. The members were directed to *choose a different color and take turns making symbols on the paper to show your feelings now.* This drawing evolved into *the large head of a smiling little boy,* with which Alvin identified (Figure 6.14). Using black, the most dominant-appearing color, he personalized the image by adding freckles to the cheeks effecting a face similar to his own. Alvin also drew two detached, floating balloons next to the face. These disconnected balloons echoed the floating tepees in his other drawing and seemed to be metaphors for his inability to appropriately connect with the group members.

The artwork confirmed the group leaders' supposition about Alvin's declining mental status. Arrangements were made through a local AIDS project for a medical and psychological evaluation and individual psychotherapy.

Figure 6.14.   Pass-around drawing

A Group Mural: Symbolic Support

An art therapy group mural can allow members a chance to symbolically give something to, and receive something from, the other participants. If used as part of a last session, the mural can help group members deal with good-byes and the issue of loss on a personal and positive note.

A three-part directive was given as follows: (1) *draw or use collage to create a symbol of yourself;* (2) *cut out the symbol and place it on the group paper;* (3) *take a turn visually connecting with the artwork of others as a way of saying good-bye.* Philip, Barry, Ronald, and Alvin participated in the group mural (Figure 6.15).

Due to his progressively weakening state, Philip could barely manage to make a self-representation in the form of the simple, colorless circle, triangle, and rectangle lightly drawn in the lower right corner of the large piece of butcher paper.

Barry then added his self-shape above Philip's drawing. He chose a photo of a man in a frozen, ice-covered winter coat, with the sun shining behind his head and a mechanical form placed over his body. Barry had difficulty accepting the bleakness of Philip's imagery. When it was time to give symbolic good-byes to each other, with permission, Barry spent considerable time filling in Philip's shapes with color. This seemed to be a symbolic attempt to restore Philip's depleted vitality. It may also have been a projection of Barry's own anxieties about death and dying and his need to be filled up. Although he spent much time connecting with Philip's design, he did not reach out to the other group members.

Ronald's mural contribution was a drawing of a star, rendered in the upper left corner with the word "forever" written on it. He tried to put the group's closure into a spiritual framework by saying "nothing ends, it all goes on forever." This was a compensating gesture to help him deal with the group's disbanding and the possibility of an early death. He related his positive feelings about the group as he created lines that stretched across the entire mural, connecting each person.

Alvin placed a drawing of himself, surrounded by jagged blocks of color, in the center of the mural, indicating his narcissism and agitation. When given specific, structured tasks, he demonstrated improved cognizance. He was able to verbalize accurate perceptions of the other members' issues rather than disrupt the group and focus on his own needs. For example, throughout the group Ronald had expressed concern about financial matters. As a parting gesture, Alvin drew several large dollar signs around Ronald's star. Through the imagery, Alvin clearly responded to Ronald's needs by "symbolically" giving him money.

Overall, this final image dramatically portrayed the group's ability to reduce their isolation by symbolically connecting with each other. The art task facilitated the giving and receiving of support and helped the members reach closure through a powerful and meaningful visual "good-bye."

Figure 6.15.   Group mural

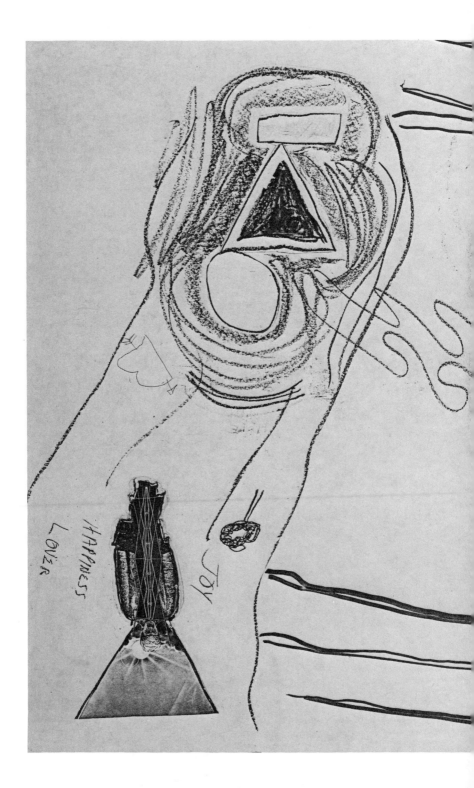

INDIVIDUAL ART THERAPY

As with group art therapy, individual work with AIDS victims can be a source of support and validation for the complicated emotional and psychological issues. The individual approach offers similar flexibility in treatment goals, time frame, and media used. For inpatients, in particular, medical restrictions will dictate media limitations. Hospitalized AIDS patients have medical stickers on their doors, identifying the need for specific precautions or isolation. When indicated, these individuals should be given separate supplies which can be disposed of when no longer needed. A psychodynamic approach is a recommended treatment method, especially because of the here-and-now issues related to this population. Following are two examples of individual work with previously mentioned group members.

Ross, the anxious resident at the AIDS shelter, was hospitalized for ulcer flare-ups. While in the hospital, he participated in an individual session, gauged to distract him from his ruminations and relieve him of some of the hospital trauma and isolation. Initially, Ross was reluctant to engage in an art task, but with support, he agreed to *choose three or four pictures that appeal to you.* An open-ended directive was given specifically because of this patient's high anxiety level and agitation.

Ross was due to leave for a trip home a month after his hospitalization. His artwork clearly reflected his focus on home and family issues. Titled "I really feild (sic) like going home," Ross chose pictures that represented security, nurturance, and family (Figure 6.16). He wrote, "Am hungry," next to a picture of wines, sweets, and nuts, which echoes his frustration with wanting to eat, but having stomach problems which made it difficult to do so without nausea. The photo of the happy family, with the caption "I miss my famile (sic)," is particularly poignant in that Ross was reared in an abusive and rejecting household. This picture reflects his wish to have a loving and accepting relationship with his mother and siblings. Ross again focused on his Midwest home with the large picture of the house, which he named "I miss being away from home." The architectural design of the photo home, however, is strikingly similar to that of the AIDS residence where Ross received consistent loving support and care. Although he did not say so, through his artwork, Ross appeared to reveal his wish to return to the safety of the AIDS shelter.

Mark, also a resident of the shelter, was the only inhabitant available for a session one day. He seemed to be in good spirits, although he appeared extremely thin and frail. The therapist and Mark explored creative options and decided to *choose different colored pens, take turns, and create a nonverbal, dual drawing together* (Figure 6.17).

Figure 6.16.   Home

Figure 6.17.   "A happy home"

Mark chose the color orange and the therapist selected pink (which shows as the lighter gray color). Mark began by drawing the stick figure in the middle left section. The therapist then "grounded" this figure with the outline of a road. In a collaborative effort, the patient and the therapist took turns adding to the drawing. Communication was through the visual imagery with the therapist providing stabilizing and nurturing lines and symbols.

At the beginning stages of the drawing, out of respect for his personal boundaries, the therapist did not "touch" any of Mark's markings. However, the therapist realized this distance, while clinically appropriate, could be a metaphor for the isolation and distancing an AIDS patient is often subjected to. The therapist began to fill in some of Mark's symbols and he responded in kind, smiling and sighing audibly when the therapist added a "gift of a kite for the stick man to play with" and "a dish of cat food for his cat." Mark appeared very pleased to have the symbolic isolation end and was reluctant to stop drawing after 50 minutes. He titled the composition "A Happy Home" and expressed his marvel at the mutual cooperation and positive results. He asked the therapist, "Did you know it would turn out like this?" This dual drawing was a powerful resource for communication, as evidenced by this meaningful session. The beneficial effects of the interaction were readily seen in Mark's improved affect. Unfortunately, Mark died three days later. Perhaps, though, this simple drawing helped him make a positive connection with another human being and allowed him to experience his creativity and worth through this visual activity.

CONCLUDING REMARKS

The art therapy modality provides people who have Acquired Immune Deficiency Syndrome (AIDS) with the chance to tap into their unconscious. They can use their creativity to help themselves cope with what their conscious mind battles to fathom, that is, terminal illness. The visual expression of personal metaphors sustains these individuals in a safe, distanced encounter with their rage and encourages them to pictorially explore ways to appropriately express and contain it. Through the use of specific symbols, people with AIDS can gradually consider and mourn multiple losses. Imagery stimulated by particular or undefined art directives can help patients find inventive ways to cope with their pain and reserve life-extending hope. When individuals and group members share their artwork with others, the feelings these powerful images communicate evoke the understanding and support that words can never convey.

REFERENCES

Buckingham, S. L., & Van Gorp, W. G. (1988). AIDS-dementia complex: implications for practice. *Social Casework: The Journal of Contemporary Social Work,* June, 371–375.

Centers for Disease Control. (February, 1990). *HIV/AIDS Surveillance Report.*

Franzino, M. A., Geren, J., & Meiman, L. (1976). Group discussion among the terminally ill. *International Journal of Group Psychotherapy, 26*(1), 43–48.

Moynihan, R., Christ, G., & Silver, L. G. (1988). AIDS and terminal illness. *Social Casework: The Journal of Contemporary Social Work, June,* 380–387.

Namir, S. (May 8, 1985). *The Psychological Impact of AIDS.* Testimony given at the hearing of the Los Angeles City/County AIDS Task Force.

Chapter 7

Termination: Theory and Practice

Helen B. Landgarten

The termination phase of therapy is a time for review, a time for separation and loss, a time for mourning, as well as a time for graduation and celebration. The dichotomous emotions of sadness and joy are experienced side by side, not only for the client but for the therapist as well.

The theme of separation is one that is dealt with consistently throughout treatment because the mourning of losses and the growth process of individuation run along parallel roads that converge with successful therapy. The termination phase is that final, mastery stretch which patients travel—the one that puts them nearer to their greater destination of autonomy and a life which contains some measure of self-fulfillment.

Singer (1961) describes the clinician's termination with the patient as analogous psychologically to the "end of parenthood." He believes it focuses the therapist's awareness of his/her own aging process. A comparison is made to the patient by Dewald (1964), as he contrasts termination to the adolescent stage of development with its struggle for emancipation, separating from the family, and shifting from dependency to independency. It is those same characteristics that also help the individual gain maturity and autonomy from the therapist.

There are various criteria for termination. For instance, Freud (1950) looked for a sufficient capacity for "enjoyment and efficiency"; while Naumburg (1953) believed the end was possible after the unconscious was brought into awareness; Blanck and Blanck (1988) watch for reasonable maximum autonomy, while Singer (1961) focuses on a striving for growth; and Menninger (1958) seeks the client's capacity for intensified relationships. The author Ortmeyer (1978) stresses self-actualization and a reduction of tension; and Szalita (1976) points to the differentiation between feeling, thought, and action and the acceptance of one's sexuality. The belief that criteria are neither possible nor appropriate is set forth by De Simone Gaburri (1985).

Consideration for introducing termination is best made by the patient after symptom resolution has proved to be lasting. Firestein (1974), Landgarten (1987), Robbins (1975), and Wolberg (1967) agree that if the patient fails to address the finalization of treatment, the therapist is obligated to bring the topic to the forefront and to interpret the patient's failure to do so. It is always preferable for patients to realize when therapy has run its course and to be ready to deal with the end of treatment and the letting-go of the therapist. Although some clients may address the issue forthright, there are also those who allude to termination as a way to test themselves and their inner responses. These latter patients tend to wonder if their hint will be picked up and how it will be perceived by the clinician. Regardless of whether or not the client is ready for termination, the innuendo should be brought forth and dealt with. The subject of termination might appear initially through a dream according to Chessick (1974). Landgarten (1981) has found that in the cases of art therapy, symbols of birthing or tree growth are frequently drawn. When the time to discontinue treatment is appropriate, the exact date can be worked out between the patient and practitioner.

There are also situations when individuals, in spite of reaching their goals or having been at a plateau for a particularly lengthy time, appear oblivious to giving cessation any thought. In these instances I will initiate termination.

The length of the termination phase varies because it is based on the intensity, number of sessions per week, and the length of treatment. Sufficient time is allotted to deal with the feelings termination evokes and to bring closure to the therapy. It is a period during which the patient's ability to walk the path of life, without help, is reaffirmed. Generally, with several years of long-term art psychotherapy, two or three months are set aside for termination. For treatment that lasts about a year to a year-and-a-half, six weeks are most effective. For short-term work that lasts anywhere from three to six months, a few weeks are required. For brief therapy or crisis intervention that takes up to three months, the beginning and end are worked upon simultaneously and an actual count down takes place. In cases of crisis intervention there is no need to deal with termination since the few art therapy sessions are devoted to the emergency at hand.

My post-therapy philosophy, whether to use the open- or closed-door policy, is evaluated according to the particular case. However, in most instances, the door is left "open." With these patients I present the "food-market" analogy (Werbach, personal communication, 1976). The individual is notified that therapy is like a grocery store—a place to fill up on emotional nourishment and growth. But after termination of therapy, there may be times when the patient needs replenishment. Under such circumstances he/she is free to return for additional supplies. Yet there are instances when my services end completely with termination. If the open door may cause regression, due to the client's belief that treatment is a symbol of dependency, then the closed door is presented. There are also cases where community resources are particularly help-ful since it gives the client a feeling of control. In utilizing these services the individual can realize that support is available in numerous places and depen-dency upon the therapist is not necessary.

A uniquely advantageous benefit of art psychotherapy is the art tasks review. This technique was originally introduced by Naumburg (1953) and is described in her book *Psychoneurotic Art: Its Function in Psychotherapy*. The recapitulation of the therapy is performed by viewing the artwork as a symbol of the patient's self-recorded treatment process. This summary takes place during the termina-tion phase, after the patient explores the feelings around bringing closure to treatment and before the final meeting.

The pacing of the review is important, since significant past memories literally stand before the patient and elicit a myriad of emotions. Confronting the evidence of one's own therapy process is a powerful, positive reinforcing agent. It is necessary and helpful for individuals to witness the pain of their past and to reaffirm their corrective and integrative experience. Therefore, for long-term cases where the art review contains a large number of significant products, as many as four sessions may be required to cover all of the impor-tant material.

After the review, during the remaining sessions, the dissolution of the transference is reinforced. When the client gives the therapist "credit" for her/his improvement, the therapist points to the collection of art, created by the client's own hands, as proof of the individual's struggles and therapy work. Such overwhelming evidence serves to diminish the residual magical powers pro-jected onto the therapist and strengthens the shift to seeing the clinician in the role of a mentor.

The last terminating session is dedicated to the final visual and oral state-ments of "good-bye." The success of the closing phase of therapy has spill-over benefits into the numerous separations and losses that will be encountered, both by the client and the therapist throughout their lives.

CASE HISTORY: MR. TATE

Mr. Tate was in art psychotherapy for a period of three years. At the age of 58 he suffered a stroke. The prognosis for full recovery from his speech impair-ment and partial paralysis of an arm and leg was questionable. Formerly a highly intelligent individual, Mr. Tate's stroke resulted in some brain damage, yet he remained within a normal range of intelligence.

Stripped of his former roles within the family, career, and social realms, the patient presented a severe depression, along with symptoms of a post-traumatic stress disorder. His three years of treatment included individual, conjoint, and family sessions.

A great deal of the therapy dealt with the patient's numerous losses. Grief and mourning took the highest priority along with self-expression. Initially, Mr. Tate withdrew from portraying any affect. His emotional life was purposely hidden at home and in therapy because of his unrealistic fear of repercussions. After a year and a half of art psychotherapy, Mr. Tate gained insight through the metaphor and began to practice new behaviors through the art tasks. This technique facilitated an appropriately open display of his thoughts and feelings.

During the third year Mr. Tate's awareness led him to work through his fears, inhibitions, misperceptions, symbiotic ties to his wife, and job-related passivity. As a result, he adapted himself to a more productive and satisfying lifestyle.

The evidence of the patient's readiness to separate from the therapist and to function autonomously was apparent when Mr. Tate began to consider an out-of-state job possibility. When he first mentioned his thoughts about a move, he discussed the issue of termination and wondered if I agreed that the time had come to end therapy. Since the goals of treatment had been accomplished and sustained, I realized that any prolongation of therapy would be due to the positive countertransference. The parting with this particular patient would be very difficult, since I admired him and was proud to treat this man who had overcome tremendous adversities. Having grown very fond of Mr. Tate, I knew it would be painful to give up seeing him and the gratification engendered in this relationship. Nevertheless, it was the correct timing for termination and an ending date was set, one that provided two-and-a-half months for the terminating phase.

Several weeks before the final meeting, Mr. Tate was informed that an *art review* would take place the following week. He was told that he would see for himself the emotional state he was in when therapy began and would witness a personally recorded *progression of his self-work*. Mr. Tate agreed to having the session videotaped, which he would view the week following the art review. This was planned to reinforce the termination and to facilitate closure.

The visual recapitulation of the treatment process is described herein. Both the patient's and my own responses are detailed in the following section.

Graphic Art Therapy Review

Mr. Tate entered the art therapy office and as he seated himself I asked if he had any special feelings about the forthcoming pictorial summary. He replied, "No, because I was concerned about a phone call from my son this morning. He wanted to know about his check. Although I answered him, I'm. . . ."

Mr. Tate was obviously prepared to go on discussing his son. However, this particular tactic was a regressive one. The patient had utilized it in the past when he chose to deflect the treatment process away from himself. Since it was necessary for the termination review to proceed, his resistance to pursuing the art summary was interpreted. Mr. Tate hesitated for a moment then admitted that he had unconsciously leaned upon his former defense of denial. He agreed to begin the recapitulation of his treatment through the art that he had created.

I explained that the pictures were arranged into two groups. The first comprised a variety of themes that were worked upon in therapy; the second group included only his drawings of people. This author, taking an educational stance, reminded Mr. Tate that an individual's psychological self-image is revealed through the way that figures are portrayed.

Thematic Artwork

As the first picture from the thematic group was propped up on the table easel, the patient mumbled, "Mmmm, mmm, boy." This particular phrase had not been uttered in the last two years. Before his full speech had returned, his limited vocabulary seemed to revert to a former stage of development. "Mmm mmm boy" and "Oh boy, oh boy" were frequently repeated and expressed his frustration and unhappiness at the time.

The picture that had been set before him caught Mr. Tate's attention. On the left side of the picture was a bound up phallic symbol with the title, "My Frustration and My Psychosis." To the right was a portrait in profile, poignantly named "My Happy One." These polarized sides indicated the split that Mr. Tate had experienced.

The recollection of those past agonizing days reminded him that he had believed his brain damage left him in a psychotic state. Mr. Tate turned his head away from the easel to make direct eye contact with me and offered his appreciation for straightening out these misperceptions. The expression of gratitude seemed to be his way of ending any discussion about that particular artwork. However, I went on to mention that the x-ed out phallus had also represented the frustration over his impotence, not only sexually, but in every area of his life. At that time he had lacked the ability to perform most of his former tasks.

I retraced Mr. Tate's past therapy, explaining that when he was convinced of his "sanity," he turned to the use of denial as a defense against facing the future realistically. He was determined to believe that he would return to his former self and would begin life where it had ended before his stroke.

The patient laughed ironically when he recalled those fantasies. Then with the full realization of his current condition, his facial expression turned to one of self-depreciation and he declared that "the stroke did result in some brain damage." Even though this was true to some extent, the patient referred to a recent intelligence test that he had taken. With a saddened look, Mr. Tate said that the results showed him to be "only average." He smiled sardonically as I commented about it being painful to see himself in that light.

As the conversation continued, Mr. Tate's current acceptance of his physical and job-related capabilities were discussed. The positive reinforcement lifted Mr. Tate's spirit and he voiced his desire to continue with the art therapy review.

Switching over to a collage, I pointed out, "This was another one of your initial tasks. It was done just before Christmas when you were told to *select any pictures of your choice* and to *record what the people in the photograph might be thinking and what they might be saying.*

The patient became sad as he looked at the photograph of a frightened little boy who was staring up at an amorphous figure. He read aloud what he had written three years previously: "the boy is thinking about fear and he is showing his fear," and "the doctor said to him, 'wait the future is great.'" I interpreted these images as the undefended way in which he revealed his feelings and wishes to me.

Flipping to the next picture, Mr. Tate viewed a dramatic collage. On one side of the page, a photo of a handsome vital looking man was pasted. The words "Myself Before" explained the picture. Next to it was a heartrending drawing of a head with all the facial features blanked out. The words above it state, "An Abstract," and below in bold print was the message, "Forsaken."

Mr. Tate became depressed as he gazed upon his artwork. It hurt him to remember that time when he saw himself as an "abstract," a "nonperson," someone who no longer existed in the fullest sense. He could barely speak as he chokingly confessed, "Sure, I felt forsaken. That's right. That's how I felt."

Before going on, I acknowledged the patient's difficulties in looking back upon himself and the painful emotions that accompanied his encounter with the past. Yet, in spite of Mr. Tate's admission to his vulnerability, he looked at me and I was stalwartly told to go on to the next picture!

He was puzzled by a collage with photos of three people: a woman, a man, and a boy. Even though he questioned me about the writing on the art, he managed to take over the control by reading what it said himself. He stated, "This man is thoughtful—perhaps nervous—and the woman is frightened, and the boy is nervous" (Figure 7.1). I pointed out that these pictures were projections of his own situation.

A dramatic magazine picture included the photograph of a man behind a glass door that displayed a sign, "Closed Due to Illness." I reminded Mr. Tate that this photograph revealed his hidden thoughts that he was still ill and possibly in a terminal state. Consultations between the physicians and myself finally made it possible for Mr. Tate to understand that his physical condition was in the process of recovery and his fears were unfounded.

To lessen his anxiety of being inundated by too many depressive images, I noted that although there had been a large amount of artwork related to his traumatic fears, they had been eliminated. Instead, a limited number of pictures were selected to typify the way in which he portrayed his thoughts and emotions. It was stressed that this type of self-expression was especially valuable, since he had refused to "chance it" by any other means of communication.

Mr. Tate, involved in the review experience, motioned to the next drawing. It was a powerful portrait of himself with a grid that blocked out his facial features except for his eyes. As the patient focused on the title, "Trying for Me,"

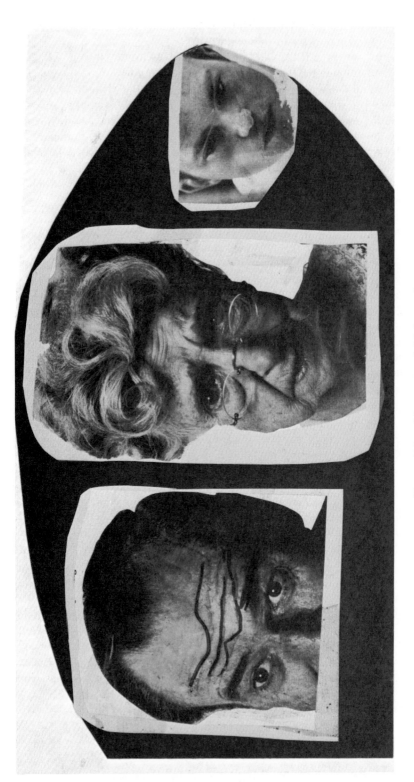

Figure 7.1.   Nervous and frightened

he was unable to recall its meaning. He was shown the words above his drawing, "Trying for Me." He struggled to bring forth the repressed memory of that feeling. Distrustfully, he looked towards me and I reminded him that in those days he was determined to keep his thoughts caged and his mouth symbolically muzzled because he was afraid to show his sadness and rage. Exposing emotions at a time when he was dependent upon others was far too threatening for him. As he recalled that period of his life, Mr. Tate became depressed. Therefore, because of my concern about "overloading" my client, we skipped over the next few similar drawings.

Nevertheless, in spite of my efforts to eliminate some of the artwork, an image of a bound-up phallus was sighted by the patient. I decided to take advantage of the silence and chose not to make any comment while I proceeded to select a photo collage. As Mr. Tate examined his art, his pained look disappeared. Figure 7.2 contained many photos: looking left to right, he was quick to recognize the first picture, which stood for a vacation he had taken with his wife. Then he remembered how the second magazine photograph had helped him to recall his hospital experience. This image had been of paramount significance because up until that time, Mr. Tate had refused to address his frightening hospitalization. The collage had provided avenues for recalling and working on the psychic trauma of that event. It was also due to this art that the patient was able to produce his first positive message. It came about via the third image of a man who was "thinking about a fabulous dinner." In addition, of utmost consequence was the last cutout of a man in a hospital bed because he identified it with the statement, "I'm hurrying toward life." This metaphoric declaration had revealed a motivation for recovery and a positive prognosis.

As Mr. Tate thought about this "hopeful" art which emerged from the dreaded past, his mood lightened and he smiled with relief. He realized that the review had finally reached the point where he was physically and emotionally on the road to recovery. Looking forward to the next picture, Mr. Tate was pleased to see his drawing of a smiling face (Figure 7.3).

It was during that particular phase of treatment that the patient's positive transference allowed him to be more trusting. I commented on the way in which he had begun to show a fuller range of emotions. For instance, he had begun to take mini risks through the art. He had started to experiment with new media and forms. Mr. Tate had used paint and markers in a nonobjective style and had demonstrated his feelings more honestly and directly. The work that illustrated these phenomena was a picture filled with blotches of color. During that phase of therapy, the patient had been told to *symbolize how you feel about the last therapy session*. I told Mr. Tate, "I knew you had been angry with me during that meeting. Never before did you permit yourself to have such feelings because up to that point you would just wipe them away. But in this painting you finally let me know some of your rageful emotions" (Figure 7.4). The patient was reminded that he had also had this same difficulty in regard to his wife. This type of confrontation had been far too frightening because of his fantasized repercus-

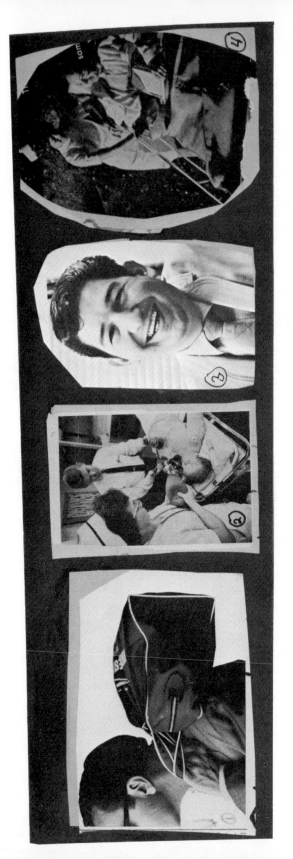

Figure 7.2.   Awareness and positive plans

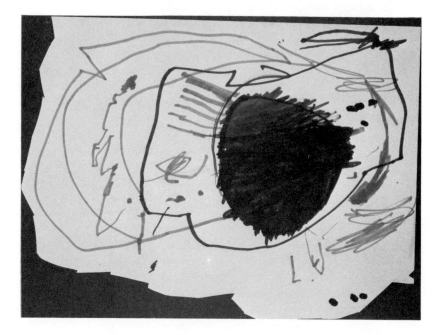

Figure 7.4. Angry

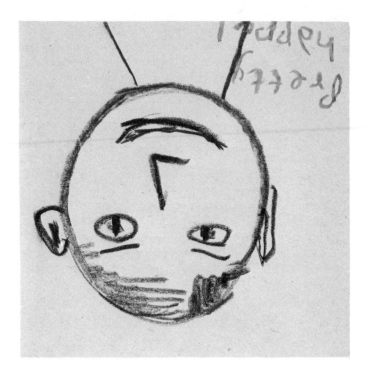

Figure 7.3. Happy

sions. These statements brought chuckles from Mr. Tate because, in retrospect, he could hardly believe that he had needed to be so careful about what he said to either his therapist or his spouse.

Because of the lateness of the hour, the next few pictures were put aside randomly. However, one of the pages caught Mr. Tate's attention. It was an ink drawing of a man in a wheelchair. He mistook its original meaning, claiming it referred to his hospital stay. I corrected this misperception, explaining that at the time it stood for his mistaken belief that if he did not behave—that is, if he gave his wife any trouble or voiced any complaints—she would place him in a convalescent hospital. The words that accompanied this drawing were "Rest and Incoherent." It represented the rest home, which he feared would turn him into an eternal invalid.

I explained to Mr. Tate that this drawing had served an invaluable purpose because his assumptions had been totally incorrect. When his wife saw the sketch, she was pained by the misunderstanding and assured her husband that she never considered such an action in the past, nor would it be an option in the future. She had sincerely encouraged her husband to share his thoughts and feelings because she believed it would help them to restore their former relationship.

The memories of his psychological work and recovery made Mr. Tate ponder the significance of his therapy. We did not speak for several minutes and there was a long pause before another picture was placed upon the easel. The next image, Figure 7.5, had been created one year later. Large in size and strongly drawn, it illustrated a woman crawling up a hill to a house with a tree nearby. It was titled "Christina" and was fashioned after a famous Andrew Wyeth painting. This picture had been created only a few months before the review and shortly after termination had been agreed upon. Mr. Tate had purposely drawn "Christina" to depict the analogy between himself and the disabled person in the painting. He had also likened her symbolic upward movement to his own emerging growth. In addition, he had free associated the "abandoned house" in the art to his own home, which would be vacated in the near future.

It was after he interpreted the person and the house that he decided to add a tree. He defined it as a "pine, an evergreen, that is really growing." Together we reminisced. We recalled our discussion about that picture and the way Mr. Tate had unconsciously produced a metaphor for his own personal growth.

In spite of Mr. Tate's realization of his vast gains, ambivalence about leaving his home and his therapist existed. I addressed the mixed emotions, aroused by the parting that was soon to take place. With his new life in a distant city getting closer, the sadness of separation and the happiness of a positive future coexisted. For a few minutes, we sat gazing at the art of "Christina," while we each turned inward to examine our own thoughts. I was dealing with my own ambivalence around termination. On the one hand, there was a loss, and on the other, was the satisfaction of a successful treatment plus the gratification of seeing a patient expand and be ready to face life realistically and bravely. Mr. Tate exhibited his

Figure 7.5.   Christina

own conflict when he sighed and questioned whether or not his rehabilitation had been completed. Yet, despite these thoughts, he went forward and turned his attention to the next collage that was being presented. The art was an update of his past, present, and future plans (Figure 7.6) with these images:

1. A magazine picture of broken glass, which stood for his past trauma. As Mr. Tate examined this photo he proudly said that although the "terror" had been horrendous he had "slowly made it through!"
2. The sketch of his brain was accompanied by the sentence, "My mind is not brilliant, but it is all I have." It was originally written with a sense of humor. When Mr. Tate read it aloud during the review, he joked that even though he was no longer "brilliant," he had finally come to grips "with this fact."
3. The photograph of a powerful design which contained strong raylike lines also had "Expand your mind" printed on it. Underneath this cut-out, Mr. Tate had written, "Slowly. . . . I work toward expansion and labor" (referring to obtaining a job). Because this sentiment was especially meaningful, Mr. Tate beamed as he read it aloud. He claimed this aspect had been resolved by his future job prospects in Florida.

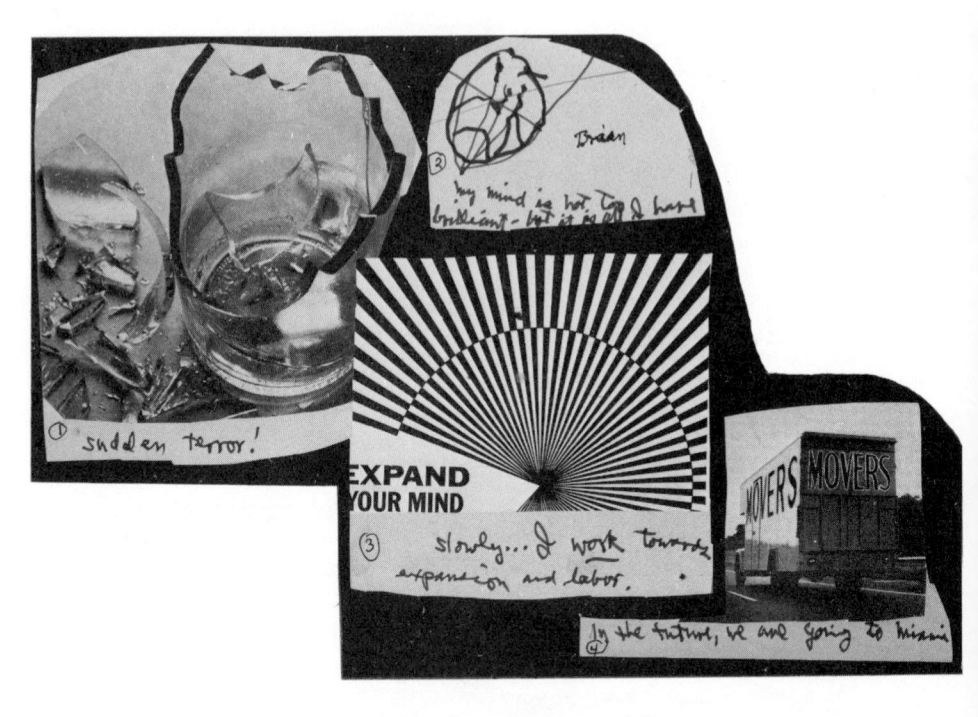

Figure 7.6.   Past, present, and future

4. Underneath the magazine picture of a moving truck driving away Mr. Tate
    had written, "In the future we are going to miami beach!" He responded
    happily to these prophetic plans and laughed at the exclamation point
    which showed the importance of this goal.

Mr. Tate recalled that initially he had refused to face his limitations. He
remembered how he kept believing that his former life would be resumed
without any changes. The patient confessed that it was only after I had con-
sulted with his physicians and had firmly stated that he would never be able to
return to his former newspaper position, that he began to deal with his situation. Mr. Tate admitted, "It finally got me in touch with reality and helped me
come to grips with life."
     Once again, the patient stopped to integrate the visual imagery in his art and
the working-through process of termination. After a while he appeared more
relaxed. He stated, "That's a nice technique that you have here." When I questioned him, "What does it do?" he replied, "It takes me back to the beginnings
[of therapy], then brings be back to the present reality." He admitted that he
had not realized "how it all fits together," and then added, "but I will think about
it." After a few moments he added, "And I will steadily go ahead."
     There was a sharp contrast between the collage that was being examined and
his first artwork before the stroke. Initially, his "past" self-image was displayed in

a winning light, powerful and successful, an "explosive type," whereas the present was a "dismal despair," "an abstract." Now, towards the end of treatment, the situation was reversed, for the "terror" of the past was put to rest and the present meant dealing with the positive aspects of his current situation.

Mr. Tate's work in art psychotherapy was so poignantly graphic that for a few minutes he appeared overwhelmed by the evidence that had been set before him. This bold confirmation of the patient's gains could not be denied. It served a supportive purpose during the termination process when severing the ties to the therapist is necessary and individuation is the paramount goal.

Figure Drawings

As I set aside the artwork that had already been discussed, another group of pictures were brought out. These were specifically contained figure drawings. Since they dramatically demonstrated the patient's psychological development, they were purposely selected for the second part of the session. This artwork contained further graphic proof of the patient's gains and was therefore ideal for bringing closure to this terminating session.

Mr. Tate was notified that an intellectual approach would be used for this second part of the review. The emphasis would be more on the way the figures were drawn, rather than on the trauma of his past. Although it remained unspoken, using this approach was a way of shifting from the patient-therapist relationship toward that of student-teacher.

Mr. Tate was pleased to leave his sufferings behind and looked forward to this new experience. The first picture (Figure 7.7) was a family sketch that he made

Figure 7.7. Instability

at the beginning of therapy. The figures were unfinished; the lower halves of the bodies were all missing. The figures were interpreted as a metaphor for the artist's perceptions of himself as well as significant others. For example, the legless family drawings revealed the instability and the uprooted state in which they existed. Mr. Tate was quick to acknowledge these facts and was eager to see the next picture.

It was a landmark piece of art for him because it was the first time a full-length figure was portrayed (Figure 7.8). The patient recognized it immediately and began to talk about its meaning. However, to keep him focused on the symbols of growth, as perceived through the "person-pictures," his attention was redirected to the projective growth clues that the images offered. Since this drawing paralleled the major strides in his life, Mr. Tate's mood lightened as he continued viewing the forthcoming artwork.

Figure 7.8.   Emotional growth

Figure 7.9.   Comparative family drawing

For comparative reasons, another family configuration was examined. Even though its appearance was robotlike, all of the body parts were included (Figure 7.9). It provided an impressive contrast from the first family picture, one that indicated that the automated type of features were analogous to the way in which Mr. Tate had functioned during that period. He was fearful of expressing himself spontaneously and he tended to react in an overly rigid fashion. Amazed and delighted at the insights that the art provided, the client was convinced of the benefits of the review.

What followed was a full-length picture of himself "feeling scared" (Figure 7.10). This sketch poignantly conveyed the patient's emotions, and the body size and details were in correct proportions and fully realized. When Mr. Tate had the courage to express himself more freely in the art, he also began to take risks with greater freedom in his communication at home. In fact, it was only a few weeks after this picture was drawn that Mr. Tate managed to tell his wife for the first time how he felt about a variety of concerns.

Fascinated by the summarizing procedure, Mr. Tate was completely involved with the process. He was delighted by the next piece of art which was a mixed-media collage. A magazine photo of a man's head had been placed on the page while the full-length figure had been sketched in (Figure 7.11). The large picture (30 inches long), was a powerful and convincing artistic statement—one that expressed the strength which the artist experienced at that stage of his development.

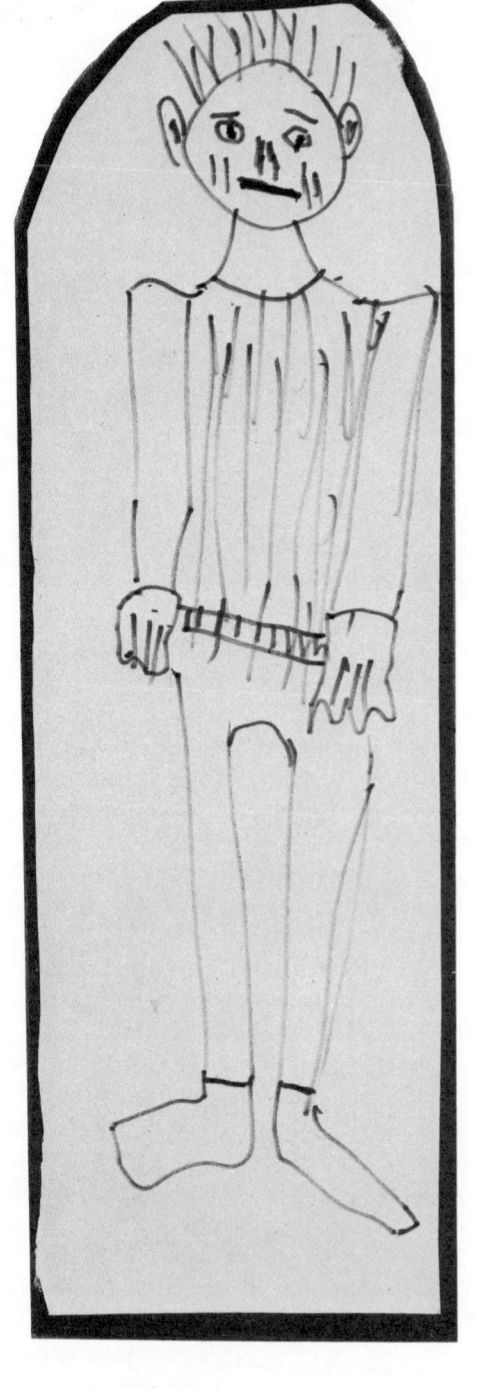

Figure 7.10.   Growth process

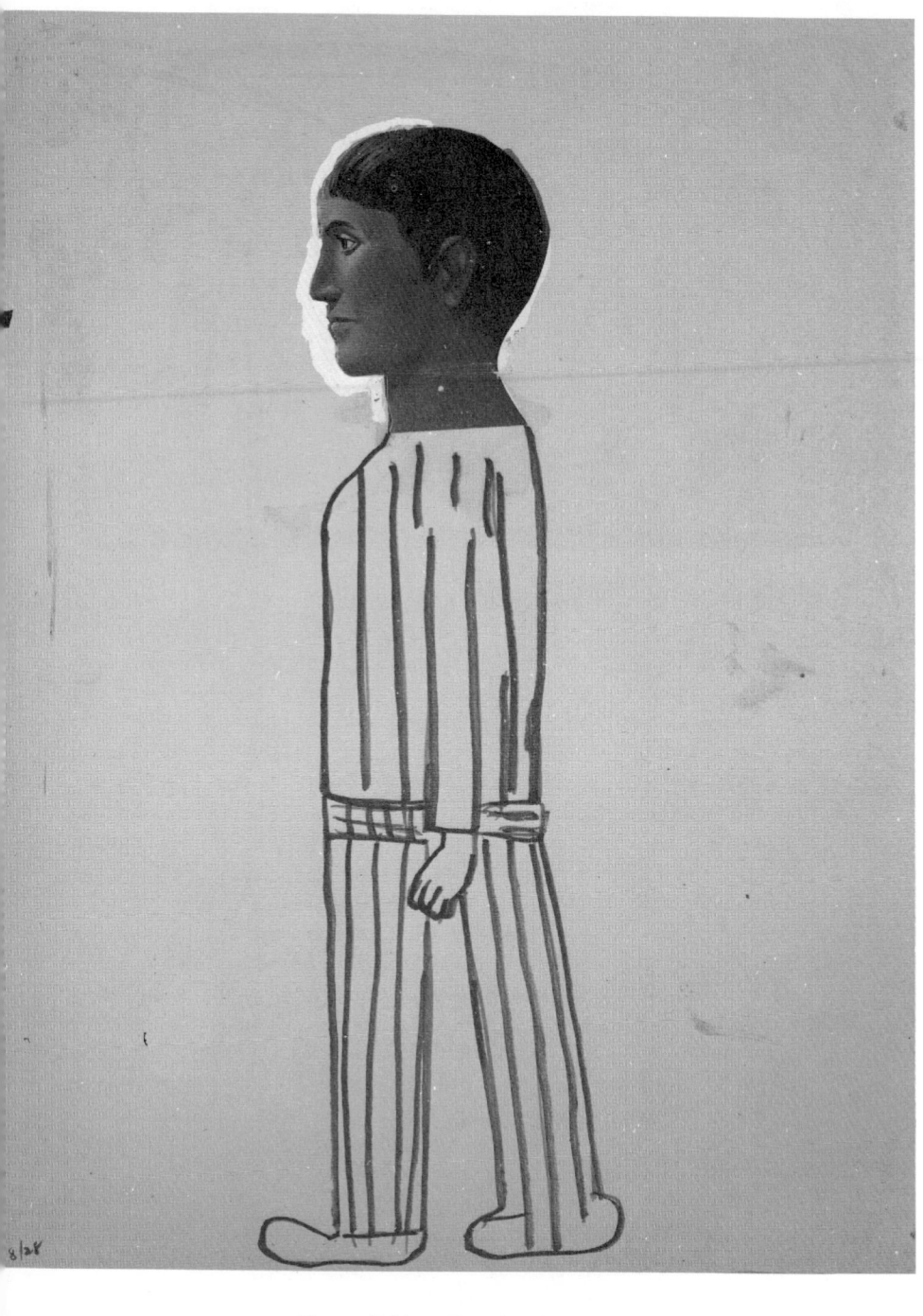

Figure 7.11.   Ego development

Figure 7.12.   Son and self

The sketch that followed was one of the patient and his son. It was regressed stylistically in a triangular manner (Figure 7.12). Because of this symbolism and the fact that the drawing was done quickly with little investment or caring, it reflected the emotional stress in their family relationship.

Most impressive because of its size and style was the next piece of art. Mr. Tate was reminded that when he had been asked to *draw something about himself,* he became inspired and was determined to create a picture that was very large. In fact, he had used two pieces of paper and glued them together to expand his space to twice the usual size. Turning to me he read aloud, "I feel calmer and more content" (Figure 7.13). We both chuckled with pleasure when we noticed the resemblance of facial features in the drawing to those of his own face. Mr. Tate again marveled at the psychological relationship between the art products and himself. He was obviously satisfied not only with the images that he had created, but also with his work both inside and outside of therapy.

The next picture was a portrait of this therapist. Mr. Tate had drawn me yelling the word "lousy" at him. "Helen" was printed beneath the quotation (Figure 7.14). When the sketch was discussed, the patient fantasized that I was also calling him "a bitch." At the time when the picture was created, Mr. Tate had been overly occupied with his physical therapy, career rehabilitation, and stroke victims group meetings. All of these activities continued beyond the point of meaning. Therefore, during the session, I interpreted his involvements as a way of avoiding the real world, which included a job. It was at that particular

Figure 7.13. Increase in self-esteem

Figure 7.14.   Therapist's portrait: angry projection

moment that my portrait was produced and purposely distorted to emphasize the anger which he projected upon me. When the displacement or projection of his own feelings were interpreted, Mr. Tate agreed. That particular experience had been a positive one because he realized that ventilating his feelings would not result in any negative action on the part of the therapist. Sensing my ego strength, he was relieved and as a result, he drew yet another portrait, one in which I appeared benign.

The last artwork (Figure 7.15) exhibited a realistic, total body image in movement, indicating that Mr. Tate was truly in touch with himself, his body, and his emotions. As he thought about the visual progression of his work and the way it culminated in these most recent projective figures, he let out a sigh of wonderment. The gesture displayed how impressed he was with his art therapy endeavors and the way it recorded his past, as well as his gains.

With the drawing summary over, Mr. Tate reached back to look over his "Forsaken" picture once again. As he did so, he was saddened. I noted aloud that it was still difficult for him to be reminded of the traumatic effect that the stroke brought about. Silently, he nodded in agreement, then took a long pause to reflect upon the pictures and the memories of his life and his therapy.

After a long while he looked around the office. He seemed to be saying good-bye to the room. Then, suddenly, he caught sight of one of his sculptures which was placed on a counter in the office. It was a plasticene skull that he had formed, and next to it was a note explaining the meaning: "I'm not able to concentrate as well as I did"; it expressed the negative side of his stroke. Yet, the positive part was printed in large and bold letters, "I'm alive." I said that the sculpture exhibited his conflict. Although he was well aware of the positive side of his life, it still hurt to think about what he had lost.

Figure 7.15.   Body image: progress and movement

Suddenly, Mr. Tate began to talk about a recent incident that occurred while attending a friend's wedding. At first it seemed as though he was diverting the attention away from the art review process. However, as he continued to speak, I realized that he was reporting a testimony to his progress. He explained that he had approached a publisher, a former employer, at the wedding. The man was astounded by the fullness of his recovery. This particular affirmation of his gain was especially significant because it came from someone who knew him in the working world. Mr. Tate went on to say that he felt "good" because of his courage in approaching the publisher.

I wondered aloud if the meeting had also stirred up some old feeling around his work. His sad affect and silence indicated that he was dealing with the losses of his past. Yet, because this issue was paramount in this meeting, I said, "Loss and parting are what we are dealing with here today. You will be leaving. Terminating. Stopping therapy. You'll be moving away. Today's session is hard in many ways." Looking downcast, Mr. Tate began to say something but then choked up. In trying to clear his throat, Mr. Tate began to cough and then left the office. I followed him to make sure he was all right, then I noticed that he was headed for the water fountain. It seemed that the break for a drink of water would also provide him with time to gather courage to face the departure from his therapist.

When Mr. Tate returned, rather than engage him in a dialogue, he was told to draw a picture. Without any hesitancy, he swiftly spilled out a forcefully sketched picture and beneath it he printed "A shark prowling about the water" (Figure 7.16). When asked to talk about the image, Mr. Tate claimed he was unaware of

Figure 7.16.   The shark: brave yet vulnerable

its meaning. Although he was gently encouraged to seek out its symbolism, Mr. Tate was resistant. He was then nudged to free associate by being reminded that he had frequently managed to interpret his metaphoric language. Still, no explanation seemed to be forthcoming.

There was a long pause before I asked him, "What does a shark remind you of?" Mr. Tate pointed to the topside of the shark with its sharp edges and explained, "It is a dorsal fin." When he was questioned about the bottom part, he pronounced it as "the underbelly." I believed that the "shark," an aggressive object, represented Mr. Tate and that his vigilance, "prowling in the water," was an appropriate response since his future was still unknown. Nevertheless, the smile shown on the shark's face represented some joy at gaining autonomy and learning to swim in a new environment. Mr. Tate pointed out the dorsal fin. Because its function is that of balance and a guide, it is plausible that his metaphor stands for Mr. Tate's ability to manage to stay steady and not to sink while on his journey to a new life. Still, his vulnerability exists, as is witnessed by the more hidden, softer, tender "underbelly" of the shark. However, the belly is also a positive symbol because it is pregnant with the introject of the therapist. All of these interpretations were not voiced by me. Instead, I continued to coax the patient to bring out underlying meaning to consciousness. In spite of my attempts, he remained inflexible.

Nevertheless, I persisted by bringing Mr. Tate face to face with the fact that he began to cough and leave the room when treatment termination was being addressed. It was upon his return that he had drawn the shark. I asked, "How would you interpret that series of events?" Even though Mr. Tate laughed at the way I had put the point across, he was still unable to respond.

To break through, I decided to try a reversal of roles. It seemed that Mr. Tate might respond to acting as the therapist. The technique did evoke insight. He pronounced, "I would think that he is drawing a shark and he is GOING OUT THERE ALONE." When I stated, "It must be frightening to be at that place," he was quick to agree. Then switching to the first person, he spoke with conviction, "But I am determined!" He continued on to say that I was an important person to him. However, he was now ready to move on with his life, one that included a job. When I stated that I was impressed with his accomplishment, Mr. Tate acknowledged his ambivalence and that it was frightening to end therapy and to make a big move. I admitted my own mixed feelings about Mr. Tate's departure. Although pleased to have had the opportunity to work with him and to have witnessed his gains, I also was sad to say "good-bye."

As the end to the session approached, I mentioned that the meeting had been emotionally demanding and that I was appreciative of Mr. Tate's ability to "stay with the experience in spite of the painful feelings it evoked." Again we recalled his clock-watching tactics when difficult material was brought up. A laugh of fondness broke out from the patient as he remembered the past. He then looked satisfied because he realized that he was able to handle the flush of memories and could also accept the progress that he had worked so very hard to obtain.

With the session over, Mr. Tate got up from the table to announce that he had brought his camera and was going to take pictures of the artwork that was around my office. This matter had been discussed the previous week as a suitable type of gift for me. Such a gesture also took Mr. Tate out of the role of the patient, making him an equal, the competent photographer, the giver. On an unconscious level the present was a transitional object for me as a reminder of his existence.

During the next session, parts of this art review were viewed since it was recorded on videotape. The process was discussed as well as the emotions and memories that it had elicited. During the final session the patient and I drew parting gifts for each other and said our final good-byes. Mr. Tate also presented me with the photographs that he had taken in a room that still held his dramatic pictorial diary, one of trauma and recovery.

CONCLUDING REMARKS

Termination is always an ambivalent experience for both the client and therapist. Because the therapeutic alliance goes beyond the session itself, a great deal of interest and caring goes into the clinical work. Helping people work through their problems brings a gratification that is most rewarding. As sad as termination is, the sense of completion is a compensatory factor that helps this therapist go through the termination process time and again.

Mr. Tate moved to another state a few days after his last art therapy session. He and his wife corresponded with me. They reported their integration into a condominium community where they were enjoying their lives. Mr. Tate offered his services to a hospital, where he did office tasks and also related to stroke victims who looked to him as a successful role model. He attended adult education classes, always with a motivation to gather new information. He and his wife were socially active. In addition, they managed to travel and most admirably continued to broaden their horizons.

The couple visited with me several times. On these occasions we reminisced and they expressed their gratitude for the art psychotherapy treatment that they had received.

Mr. Tate died in his sleep at the age of 76. His wife continues to write to me since I represent the person with whom they shared the horrendous difficulties in overcoming the traumatic effect of Mr. Tate's stroke.

The art therapy review was valuable not only for my client but for me as well. As the artwork was revealed step by step, I could see the entire course of treatment laid out. It gave me the chance to recapitulate my client's struggle towards integration and autonomy, and afforded me the opportunity to see the part that I, as a clinician, played in Mr. Tate's life.

REFERENCES

Blanck, G., & Blanck R. (1988). The contribution of ego psychology to understanding the process of termination in psychoanalysis and psychotherapy. *Journal of American Psychoanalytic Association. 36*(4), 961–984.

Chessick, R. P. (1974). *Intensive Psychotherapy*. New York: Jason Aronson.

De Simone Gaburri, G. (1985). On termination of the analysis. *International Review of Psychoanalysis, 12,* 461–468.

Dewald, P. (1964). *Psychotherapy as a Dynamic Approach*. New York: Basic Books, Inc.

Firestein, S. (1974). Termination of psychoanalysis of Adults: A review of the literature. *Journal of American Psychoanalytic Association, 22,* 873–892.

Freud, S. (1950). Analysis terminable and interminable. *Collected Papers,* Vol. V., pp. 316–357. London: Hogarth Press.

Landgarten, H. B. (1981). *Clinical Art Therapy: A Comprehensive Guide*. New York: Brunner/Mazel.

Landgarten, H. B. (1987). *Family Art Psychotherapy: A Clinical Guide and Casebook*. New York: Brunner/Mazel.

Menninger, K. (1958). *Theory of Psychoanalytic Techniques,* pp. 155–189. New York: Basic Books, Inc.

Naumburg, M. (1953). *Psychoneurotic Art: Its Function in Psychotherapy*. New York: Grune & Stratton.

Ortmeyer, D. H. (1978). End phase of treatment. *Psychoanalytic Psychotherapy,* pp. 149–172. Reading, MA: Addison Wesley.

Robbins, W. S. (1975), Termination: Problems and techniques. *Journal of American Psychoanalytic Association, 23,* 166–176.

Singer, E. (1961). *Key Concepts in Psychotherapy*. New York: Random House.

Szalita, A. B. (1976). On termination. *Contemporary Psychoanalysis, 12,*(3) 342–347.

Wolberg, L. (1967). *The Technique of Psychotherapy* (2nd edition, part I). New York: Grune & Stratton.

Index